The UNBELIEVABLE

The UNBELIEVABLE

The Ultimate Book of
World Records and the
People who Pursue Them

**All Records Compiled and Verified
by Record Holders Republic**

David R. Adamovich, Ed.D.

Thomas Blacke

Dean Gould

Bartleby Press
Washington • Baltimore

Library of Congress Control Number: 2009940683
ISBN: 978-0-910155-77-9

Cover illustration and design by Ralph Butler

Printed in the United States of America

Published and distributed by:

Bartleby Press
8600 Foundry Street
Mill Box 2043
Savage, Maryland 20763
800-953-9929
www.BartlebythePublisher.com

Contents

Foreword

This is your life... What are you going to do about it? In the 1950s, a TV show called *This is Your Life* was hosted by Ralph Edwards. It was a documentary in which the host would surprise an unsuspecting celebrity. Before a live TV audience, the biography would unfold as family, friends, and old acquaintances would recall significant moments, often funny and sometimes tearful.

But that was *then*. What about *now*? An economic downturn has occurred and even successful people are heading for pawnshops. A record number of homes are going into foreclosure and the ability to find a job is nearly impossible. Life is filled with challenges. There is light at the end of the tunnel, however.

So what is the *hidden message* in *Believe the Unbelievable*? It's quite simple. You're about to read not just records, but the life stories and incredible motivations of those who set records. Rebuilding one's financial life in an economic downturn holds its parallels to those seeking to set or break a world record. I'm down here... Could it get any worse? I want to be up there... How have others done it?

Read carefully the backgrounds and motivations of the over 50 record holders profiled in *Believe the Unbelievable.* There are many lessons to learn in their struggles to be the best. Whether you are in the Olympics or in business, minutes, and sometimes seconds, count. Donald Trump mentioned in his book, *Think Like a Billionaire*, that I had exactly three minutes to make my pitch. He was extremely busy that day and not particularly in the mood for a presentation. He thought I would decline, thus freeing up his day a bit. Not only did I not decline, I gave him such a great presentation that we became partners. It's surprising what people can do with a deadline, even one as short as three minutes. Time is valuable. We must give ourselves a deadline, set the highest possible goal, and do our best to make our dream come true.

After more than 20 years of running a series of entrepreneurial marathons, from the Elite Brazil to Trump Realty Brazil, I have learned from my mentors, John Casablancas and Donald Trump, that if you really want to win in business and life and eventually set a record, you have to... *Believe the Unbelievable.*

Ricardo R. Bellino
Author, *You Have Three Minutes!*
Donald Trump's "First Apprentice"
World's Fastest Multimillion Dollar Deal-maker
Motivational Coach, Record Holders Republic

Preface

I formed Record Holders Republic (RHR) in 2001 to give human achievement record holders an alternative to Guinness World Records™. With Guinness' rapid growth came a proliferation of collection, tallest, smallest, etc. type of records. In turn, it became increasingly difficult to keep up with long delays in the verification process, not to mention researching current records. It could take several months to find out if a record was accepted, refused for an unspecified reason, or already beaten. Growth was taking its toll. The need for a new record organization with a different vision in verifying and reporting human achievement records was needed. RHR was created *by* record holders *for* record holders. Its mission is to create a niche market serving the specific needs of human achievement record holders.

The difficulty and frustration often encountered in searching the Guinness database was not to occur with RHR. For example, a search for a known record on their site usually results in "No records found," with the option to pay for the results via text message!

In contrast, RHR maintains an active and up-to-date, searchable database under the direction of Nick Claydon of Unicorn Designers, *http://unicorndesigners.co.uk*. RHR researchers update and upload records immediately upon verification. If the record exists, it's there and it's free.

An important milestone on the road to today was my invitation to the 1996 World Record Festival in Germany held by Ralf Laue, record historian, record breaker, and president of *http://recordholders.org*. Ralf and I would often meet each other at world record events, and within just 2 years of RHR's beginning, we collaborated on a follow-up to Mike Barwell's *The Alternative Book of Records*, creating *The Book of Alternative Records* (BOAR) by Ralf Laue and Philip Gould. RHR began to grow rapidly and more help was needed to take us to the next level.

That help came when I met (The Rev. Dr.) David Adamovich, a professional knife thrower who performs as "The Great Throwdini," the world's fastest and most accurate knife thrower. On the heels of what was initially a frustrating experience with Guinness, David turned to RHR and BOAR to validate records he was setting during performances of his Off-Broadway show, *Maximum Risk—World Champions on the Edge!* (SoHo Playhouse, NYC).

Both RHR and BOAR took interest in his knife throwing accomplishments and records. His enthusiasm and drive led to him becoming RHR's United States President.

One of David's ideas was to organize RHR's "World Records of Magic Show" at Fantasma Magic in NYC. Both television and print media were there to witness the event. A number of magicians and variety entertainers both set and broke world records. It was at this show that the next member of the RHR team was added. Thomas Blacke, an internationally known magician and escape artist, set three world records that day. David subsequently asked him to become RHR's United States Vice President. Thomas' position as International President of Escape Masters—the International Association of Escape Artists, and editor/publisher of *Escape Masters* magazine, was instrumental in finding Bartleby Press, the publisher for *Believe the Unbelievable.*

Another of his ideas was to organize RHR's Record Breakers World Cup. Together with David and Thomas, the event became a reality in April 2007, with several countries involved over 100 records were either set or broken. With our database growing, the time was right to take BOAR to the next level but this time with a focus on human achievement records only. Thus, *Believe the Unbelievable* was born.

Believe the Unbelievable: The Ultimate Book of World Records and the People who Pursue Them, focuses exclusively on human achievement records. Our records come from all corners of the world and have been authenticated by either RHR, BOAR, or affiliated organizations such as the International Sword Swallowers Association (ISSA), *The Asia Book of Records*, the International Federation of Competitive Eating (IFOCE), the National Duckpin Bowling Congress, and the American Yo-Yo Association. We anticipate that *Believe the Unbelievable* will set the standard for human achievement world records, inspiring the reader to also become a record holder.

It would be inappropriate to ignore the accomplishments and path laid by Guinness in establishing themselves as the foremost and largest world record organization. Under the leadership of Craig Glenday, Editor of their book, and Marco Frigatti, Director of Records, they continue to forge forward and grow. Even though we have nothing but respect for their organization, RHR in collaboration with BOAR expect *Believe the Unbelievable* will become the authority on human achievement world records.

On behalf of the entire Record Holders Republic team, I wish you the best of luck in all your world record attempts.

Dean Gould

Founder and President,
Record Holders Republic
www.recordholdersrepublic.co.uk

Acknowledgments

Our first and foremost acknowledgment goes to the almost 700 records holders who have contributed their efforts in approximately 1,400 human achievement records listed herein. Without their vision to be *the best in the world* we'd have little to write about.

In particular, prolific record holders such as Paddy Doyle, John Evans, and Peter Dowdeswell, with over 200 records between them, show a profile in determination and vision that serves as an inspiration to the first-time record breaker.

The RHR Team thanks Ralf Laue of the Book of Alternative Records (BOAR), a sister organization of RHR, for authenticating and contributing many of the records contained in *Believe the Unbelievable.*

A special thank you to our publisher, Jeremy Kay,

who right from the beginning knew the project had merit. He hit the nail right on the head when he said, "The records are for the people and by the people. We need a way to inspire anyone and everyone who wants to set or break a record, and provide the vehicle to do it. I *Believe the Unbelievable.*"

Thank you to associate editor Morgan Young, who typeset, copy edited, and put up with an endless number of last minute updates. Her efforts have made *Believe the Unbelievable* as up-to-date as possible before going to press.

Our efforts were supported by Barbara Adamovich and Eric Sears, who read and reread the records and converted many from metric units of measure to the foot-pound system.

 Onboard as resident "Artoonist" for Record Holders Republic is Sean Hopkins, a native of Queens, New York. An alumnus of the famed Fiorello H. La Guardia High School in NYC, he has dabbled in the fine arts for most of his life. Sean is also a published photographer as well as an accomplished musician. He is thrilled to have been given the opportunity to meet and work with David Adamovich, and proud to have his work featured in this book. To see more of his artwork as well as other projects, visit *www.SeanHopkinsArt.Weebly.com.*

Acknowledgments

Thanks to Nick Claydon, our web designer, for dealing with the uploads and many modifications along the way to get it "just right." His job, however, has just begun.

Although no longer with us, three people have contributed significantly to where we are today. They are Norris and Ross McWhirter, and Roy Castle. Each played a prominent role in the world of record breakers.

Finally, a big thank you to the entire RHR team of vice presidents and professional advisory panel.

Disclaimer

Attempting to set or break a world record may carry with it the risk of danger, property damage, bodily harm or death. All such risks are undertaken at the sole responsibility of the participant(s). Neither the authors, contributors, the publisher, Record Holders Republic (RHR), *Believe the Unbelievable* nor The Book of Alternative Records shall assume any responsibility or liability. Accepting a submission does not obligate the authors, contributors, the publisher, Record Holders Republic (RHR), *Believe the Unbelievable* or The Book of Alternative Records to accept the record for world record status nor does it promise the record shall appear in print or on Web sites owned or controlled by the authors, contributors, the publisher, Record Holders Republic (RHR), *Believe the Unbelievable* or The Book of Alternative Records.

Introduction

Records are made to be broken…except mine, that is.
—Simon Lovell,
world record holder in card shuffling

Alas, the immortal words of every world record holder as they kick and scream at the news that *their* record has been *broken*. Yes, you heard correctly—broken, as are their hopes, dreams and egos of being numero uno, King-of-the-Mountain, or whatever superlative identifies them as *the best in the world*. And so goes the cycle of setting, breaking and re-breaking world records by perhaps tenths, hundredths, even thousandths of a second.

World records are, to paraphrase Lincoln, "Of the people, by the people, and for the people." World record holders come from every possible walk of life—they belong to the young and old, male and female, beginners (a young girl from Massachusetts, Madeline Barnes, who decides on her own she is going to make the world's smallest origami fortune teller) and professional record breakers (Paddy Doyle, for example, who sets and breaks fitness and endurance records as often as someone else goes for a walk in the park.)

Believe the Unbelievable is not just a book of world records. In particular, it is about human achievement records versus collections or the tallest bridge or shortest bridge in the world. Even more importantly, it is *about the people* who set and break world records. *Believe the Unbelievable* honors their achievements and encourages anyone and everyone "of the people" to be a world record holder. Don't forget, there are only two ways to a world record: you either set one or break one. This book will tell you what drives and motivates record breakers. You'll read their profiles which highlight their personal stories, dreams and accomplishments.

Who certifies world records?

There are a number of organizations that authenticate (review documentation) and certify (attest and confirm) world records—the most famous, of course, is Guinness World Records™. However, there *are* others:

• *Believe the Unbelievable,*
• Record Holders Republic, "Registry of Official World Records,"

• The Book of Alternative Records (BOAR), and
• The World Record Federation.

These are some of the major players. Some records in *Believe the Unbelievable* have been verified by other authorities and subsequently certified by Record Holders Republic. Such authorities include the International Federation of Competitive Eating (IFOCE), the Sword Swallowers Association International (SSAI), the American Yo-Yo Association, and *The Asia Book of Records*. They have done extensive research on their own and have conducted their own festivals and events in which world records have been set and broken. We thank them for participating with Record Holders Republic and BOAR.

Does it cost anything to register my world record attempt?

Yes and no. *Believe the Unbelievable*, Record Holders Republic, and BOAR do not charge to authenticate and certify a world record. Guinness, on the other hand, has an optional fast-track/review fee of $800 (this includes the initial application and review of subsequent evidence). The fee is $600, on the other hand, if only an expedited review of the supporting evidence of the record attempt is requested. The World Record Federation charges an annual membership fee of $50. *Believe the Unbelievable*, Record Holders Republic and BOAR do not charge a fee to review or validate a record claim. All validated records appear without charge on the respective online databases and in this book.

How does Believe the Unbelievable differ from the others?

Guinness, for example, has over 40,000 records—of which human achievement records are only a small part of the database. *Believe the Unbelievable* and Record Holders Republic are exclusively human achievement records. BOAR maintains an extensive library of collection records in addition to a human achievement archive. The National Broadcasting Company aired the *Top 100 Guinness World Records™ of All Time* show in January 2008. Many Record Holders Republic and BOAR record holders appeared on Guinness' list in addition to many other non-human achievement records. The bottom line here, we're all different but all alike. The factor that remains the same in all organizations is the reporting of world records. As discussed in other places herein, there are duplications of records between organizations and where there is a difference, it's because the same record may have been broken and reported to only one organization or there are differences between the records.

Why aren't I listed in your book?

Do we know about you? *Believe the Unbelievable* does not solicit world records. Someone must make a formal application and submit verifying documents to be considered for world record status of their achievement. Likewise, the same goes for Record Holders Republic, BOAR, the World Record Federation, and Guinness. Each organization has its own set of rules to follow. Being accepted by one organization does not mean your record attempt will be of any interest to the others.

Does the same record have different values with different organizations?

Of course. Some records are cross-referenced in both because of dual submission and have the same time or quantity. On the other hand, some records are significantly different in quantity despite having the same record name. Much depends on the particular rules and regulations of the organization or perhaps the particular reviewer assigned at the time of record submission.

For example, Dr. David Adamovich aka "The Great Throwdini," tried for 3 years to have Guinness certify his record for "Most Knives Thrown Around a Human Target in One Minute: 97." They declined without reason. Two years afterward, they accepted the same record by German knife thrower Pat Brumbach, who threw 96 knives (one *less* than Adamovich) on a Guinness TV special. Dr. Adamovich resubmitted his record and it was finally accepted as breaking Patrick's 96. Subsequently, Brumbach and Adamovich broke the record an additional two times, upping the ante to 99 and then 102. As fate would have it, NBC was in the process of finalizing selections for their production of the *Top 100 Guinness World Records™ of All Time*. Dr. Adamovich's record of 102 was selected to appear in the show.

While his initial record attempt was in limbo

with Guinness, Dr. Adamovich submitted an even higher record of "Most Knives Thrown Around a Human Target in One Minute: 144," to Record Holders Republic. It was documented and approved, and to this day remains an exclusive RHR record out of respect for bypassing his deadlock with Guinness. The moral of the story, "*Don't give up*." If you've got a record worthy of being recognized, then stick to your guns and present your case with the idea that someone will listen in one organization or another and make an informed decision. Similar stories abound in the world of record setting.

How do I become a record holder?

As stated throughout, there are two ways to be a world record holder: set one and create the record *or* break an existing record. Setting a record becomes a matter of interest to the organization you are submitting your request to. It is not uncommon for a record request to be turned down for safety reasons or lack of interest. For example, someone requesting to set a record for the highest free-fall without a parachute might be told to have his or her head examined rather than, "We anxiously await the result of your record attempt."

Breaking a record is often the best way to go. There are a variety of record books available to see what's been done already. Look one up, contact the organization that cites the record, advise them of your intent, request a copy of the rules used by the current record holder and *go for it*. The most important thing to remember is documentation, documentation, and documentation. Generally speaking, this includes: a description of the event, the rules followed, how it is measured, witness statements, and if possible, video/DVD documentation. Sometimes not everything is available but the overall strength of the other components can carry a favorable decision.

Record holders may do stupid things but hopefully they are not stupid in doing them. Safety precautions must always be considered. No organization takes any responsibility for anything you do. *You* are totally responsible for your own actions, your own safety and the safety of those around you. Don't let the words of Forrest Gump stray too far from mind when thinking about a record attempt, "Stupid is as stupid does."

Whom do I contact?

Once again, it pays to submit your record to more than one organization in the event you are of more interest to one versus the other. To submit your material to *Believe the Unbelievable* or Record Holders Republic, "Registry of Official World Records," please visit *www.recordholdersrepublic.com* or go to *www.recordholdersrepublic.co.uk*. To submit to *The Book of Alternative Records*, please visit *www .alternativerecords.co.uk*. The founder of *The Book of Alternative Records*, Ralf Laue, has added the following:

"Several records in this book have been provided by the editors of *The Book of Alternative Records*. They have run an archive concerning unusual world records since 1980. You too could have what it takes to become a record breaker. No matter how great or small, we will consider your record for inclusion in *The Book of Alternative Records*. On our Web site, you can also find information about the process of record verification as well as record submission forms in several languages. However, please contact us before going for a world record. If a record is not published in this book, it does not necessarily mean that there is no current record. If you wish to find out the current status of a world record or you are considering a record attempt, whether it is an existing record or a new category of record, please contact us in the first instant. In some cases, we will send you detailed rules for the record category.

Records should be measurable and achievable. Records that are 'first' or 'only' will not be included, as these are not records that can be beaten. The record should be absolute. Age/class restricted records or national records are not considered. Special women's records will be considered only in some sports. Records for the most people doing something at the same place will only be considered if the common activity is a rather difficult one ('the most people eating fire') or produces a result (for example, 'most people playing an accordion' results in a piece of music—or at least a noise—whereas the most wearing a red nose achieves no such result).

We do not publish records that are against the law ('youngest person to drive a car on a public street'), dangerous or unhealthy ('drinking most beer within

24 hours') or just tasteless ('eating earthworms'). A record category should not be too special. For example, the 'longest banner' will be welcome, but 'the longest banner with Bible texts written by children' would be far too special. Largest collections would be welcome but duplicate items do not count for this kind of record. Largest and smallest objects must be fully operational. For example, it must be possible to play the smallest piano. They should be made from the same materials as the original object. Largest food items can be made in different parts but the final product must look like a single item. Just laying together many cakes on a table does not count as the largest cake. There are many, many records to try. Use your imagination and the records in this book as a guide. Before attempting any of the records above or within the book, please contact us for more information."

What is the difference between a world record holder and a world champion?

Tyson Gay won the 2007 World Track-and-Field Championship in the 100-meter dash with a time of 9.85 seconds. The current world record, however, belongs to Usain Bolt who, during the 2009 World Championships in Berlin, reset the world record at 9.58 seconds. World champions are often crowned on a yearly basis. In the case of the 100-meter dash, for example, the winning time may be slower than it was at any other time or even the defending time. The 100-meter world record, on the other hand, will always remain the fastest time on record until broken. Stated another way, the next ten upcoming world track-and-field championships may crown a new world champion in the 100-meter dash, all slower than 9.58 seconds. Until someone does 9.57 seconds or less, Usain Bolt shall remain numero uno, *the* world record holder in the 100-meter dash, and without question, *the* fastest man in the world.

The distinction between world record holder and world champion is further evidenced in the speed throw event held in the knife throwing world championship competition. The winning time, and the organization's record, is 22 knives thrown in 20 seconds. The world record time for the same number of knives is 9.98 seconds. World championships are contests between contenders. The fastest person wins and might very well be dethroned in one year. World records are an individual's contest with him/herself. The fastest recorded time remains just that, forever, and until broken...*the* world record.

There's an old saying that goes something like, "There are those that make things happen, those that watch what happened, and those who have no idea of what happened." Sit back and enjoy reading the stories and accomplishments about *the* people that *make* it happen...better than anyone else in the world—record breakers. These are their stories.

Chapter 1
Strength

S trength is measured in our ability to use muscles in conjunction with tendons, ligaments, and bones, acting in a coordinated effort to push, pull, lift, or press a heavy object. Like other physical attributes, raw physical strength is both inherent and subject to the outcome of daily and long-term exercise.

Skeletal muscles do the work we tell them to do. There are limitations between people based on the distribution of two types of muscle fibers, type I (slow twitch) and type II (fast twitch), both the result of genetic inheritance. It's quite fair to say that some people are born turtles (relatively weaker and suited for endurance) and others are born rabbits (relatively stronger and suited for speed). Much of this inherited quality is based on the percentage of muscle fiber type present and then, of course, on how much training the individual does to make the best of what he or she has.

Airplane Pulling

Airbus 321: 78 tons: 20 meters: 10 seconds. Franz Muellner.

Bungee Holding

Greatest Force
5 *gs*: Franz Meullner. The jumper weighed 198 lb. and jumped from a height of 223 feet as Franz held the bungee cord with his hands only.

Bus Pushing

Double Decker Bus with Head
½ mile: 15 minutes, 17 seconds. Walter Cornelius.

Cannonball Pushing

1 Mile with Nose
On March 1, 1986, Reg Morris pushed a cannonball (a 16 lb. shot) using only his nose, around Walsall, West Midlands, United Kingdom, for a distance of 1 mile (1.6 km) in exactly 42 minutes. BOAR

Fastest 50 yards
30.16 seconds. At the Alternative Olympics held in Hull, Humberside, on September 20, 1988, Pete Dowell of the Multex Mentals team won the 50 yard cannonball push with the record time of 30.16 seconds. BOAR

Car Holding

Wheelie
Ferrari Modena: 13.45 seconds. Franz Muellner.

Thomas Blackthorne

Migrates between Edinburgh, London, and Milan.
Sideshow performer and sword swallower.
Web: www.blackthorne.it
E-mail: thomas.gn@blackthorne.it

2 World Records:

Heaviest weight lifted with the tongue: 12 kg

Heaviest object sword-swallowed:
38 kg demolition hammer

Thomas Blackthorne has been working as an entertainer, in one form or another, for about 25 years. Recently, some of his more extreme acts have been recognized as world records. Thomas has quadrupled the original record for lifting weights with the tongue, and every year he travels to another country, adds half a kilo and attempts to break his record again. In England, Germany, and Italy, the lifts went without a problem, but he knows that one day he might discover his tongue's breaking limit and will have to stop. Part of the appeal of this record is the audience knows each attempt may be his last.

A few months ago, Thomas swallowed a large pneumatic hammer weighing 38 kilograms, which had to be lifted above his head with an engine hoist. When fully lowered, the weight was supported entirely on his front teeth—and the drill was left running throughout! This is Thomas' most extreme record to date and it took a while to recover fully, but it is also the most rewarding. Said Thomas about the record, "When you have spent so long planning and developing an idea, then faced the pain and danger of carrying it through, you feel so alive!"

Car Pulling

Furthest with Beard
42.65 feet. In July 2002, Lithuanian brewer Antanas Kontrimas attached an army jeep (including 5 passengers) weighing almost 3 tons to his beard with straps, pulling it a distance of 42.65 feet (13 m). Antanas, aged 50, has not shaved for over 25 years and his beard measures more than 50 centimeters in length. BOAR

Furthest with Ear
46 feet. Nadeem Raja Khan pulled a Murati 46 feet using his ears alone. ASIA BOOK OF RECORDS

Furthest with Eye
13 feet 3 inches. Ramjan Sayyed. This is achieved with string attached from eye to car, and the car is pulled toward him. ASIA BOOK OF RECORDS

Concrete Blocks

Broken with Bowling Ball on Head
6. John Ferraro aka "Gino Martino," placed six 2 x 8 x 16 inch cement blocks on top of his head with ½ x 4 inch spacers between. The cement blocks were smashed by a 14 lb. bowling ball.

Broken with Sledgehammer on Head
4. John Ferraro aka "Gino Martino," placed four 2 x 8 x 16 inch cement blocks on top of his head. The cement blocks were smashed by a 9 lb. sledgehammer.

Most Broken on Back
10. John Ferraro aka "Gino Martino," had 10 cinder blocks with a combined weight of 463 lb. placed in 2 stacks of 5 each on his back. Each stack of 5 was

broken with 5 hits by a 9 lb. sledgehammer for a total of 10 hits.

Smashed on Bed of Nails
43. George McArthur aka "George the Giant," had broken upon his chest, whilst lying on a bed of 12 inch spikes with 2½ inch spacing, 43 concrete blocks weighing a total of 1,387 lb. The blocks were 6 x 2½ x 12 inches. Broken blocks were pushed away and sledging continued until all blocks were broken.

Smashed on Chest (multiple hits)
16: 5.35 seconds. Fred Burton. Bricks were made of Durox Superblock, weighing 14 lb. each and measuring 625 x 70 x 200 centimeters. These blocks are 25 percent stronger then any other similar block.

16: 11.88 seconds. Fred Burton had 16 concrete blocks (each weighing 14 lb. and measuring 18 x 9 x 4 inches) smashed on his chest, all stacked at one time and broken with multiple smashes with a sledgehammer by one person.

32. Fred Burton had 32 concrete blocks (each weighing 14 lb. and measuring 18 x 9 x 4 inches) for a total weight of 448 lb., smashed on his chest, all stacked at one time and broken with multiple smashes with a sledgehammer by one person.

Thickest Broken on Head
8 inches. John Ferraro aka "Gino Martino," placed an 8 x 12 x 18 inch cement block on his head, without the use of a towel, and had it smashed in half by a 10 lb. sledgehammer on May 20, 2007 in Worcester, MA, USA.

Fred Burton
"The Cheadle Hercules"

63-year-old male.
Cheadle, UK.
Married with one daughter.
Professional strongman.
E-mail: fred_burton@hotmail.co.uk

Multiple Strength World Records. Among them:
16 concrete blocks smashed on chest
with multiple hits: 5.35 seconds

Fastest hot water bottle bursting: 35.6 seconds

Most dips on parallel bar in 1 minute: 32

Most weight lifted with teeth: 112 lb.

Most weight lifted with 1 finger: 252 lb.

Fred Burton is known as "The Cheadle Hercules," and in nearly 30 years, he has smashed dozens of world records. His aim is to beat as many world records as possible. He loves pushing himself to the limit of the pain barrier. Fred is 63 years old and has no intention of quitting record breaking. One of his favorite records is blowing up a hot water bottle until it bursts. The President of RHR, Dean Gould, witnessed this record. When Dean stopped the watch at 35.6 seconds, neither Dean nor Fred could believe the record had been smashed in such a great time.

Fred was 15 years old when he first discovered his strength while working at a quarry bagging clay. One day, a colleague failed to turn up for work and Fred was left on his own to fill a large shed with all these bags, which he did by lifting them all by himself. In the morning, Fred's boss arrived and could not believe he lifted them all on his own. Both Fred and his boss stood there watching three men struggling with each individual bag, trying to load them onto the lorry.

Dips

1 dip: 112 lb. weight on back. Fred Burton.

1 minute: 15-inch bench: 96. Stephen Buttler.

1 hour: 15-inch bench. 2,116. Stephen Buttler.

1 minute: Parallel bar: 32. Fred Burton.

1 hour: Parallel bar: 1,011. Craig Caesar.

Female Records
5 minutes: 75. Parallel bar. Alicia Weber. BOAR

Most: 15. Time: 1 minute. Parallel bar. Weight: 20 kilograms. Jess Jones.

Ear Lifting

With 1 Ear
143 lb. Zafar Gill of Pakistan, lifted a weight of 143 lb. (65 kg) hanging from a clamp attached to his ear, 10 centimeters above the ground. May 1, 2008 in Turkey.

Hair Pulling

Car
5,020 lb. Cynthia Morrison aka "The Great Cind-indi," pulled a 1983 Rolls Royce Corniche weighing 5,020 lb. (2.51 tons) a distance of 84 feet with a rope attached to her hair.

Truck
6,126 lb. Cynthia Morrison aka "The Great Cindini," pulled a 2008 Chevrolet Silverado pickup truck and driver a distance of 112 feet 4.5 inches with her hair looped through a metal ring attached to a towrope.

Head Balancing

Auto (Chevrolet)
352 lb. John Evans.

Auto (Mini Cooper)
356 lb. John Evans.

Beer Kegs
11. John Evans.

Boat
352 lb. John Evans.

Bookcase
John Evans.

Bunk Beds
2 sets (4 beds), 12 feet 8 inches high. John Evans.

Cans of Soft Drinks
429 cans (381 lb.) John Evans.

Cement Mixers (2)
349 lb. John Evans.

Column of Guinness Books
62: 217 lb., 48-7/8 inches. John Evans.

Column of My First Car Books
204: 287 lb., 49-1/8 inches. John Evans.

Dim Sum Steam Baskets
400 pieces. John Evans.

Flag Pole
22 feet. John Evans.

John Evans
The World's Greatest Head Balancer

61-year-old male.
Derbyshire, UK.
Married with two children.
Professional head balancer.
Web: www.headbalancer.com
E-mail: strongman@btconnect.com

35 World Records. Among them:

Most house bricks balanced on head:
101 for 10 seconds

Most milk crates balanced on head:
96 for 10 seconds

Most beer kegs balanced on head:
13 for 10 seconds

Balanced Mini Cooper on head: 10 second

Balanced juggler on head: 72 seconds

John Evans started head balancing at the age of 17

while working on a building site carrying bricks up ladders to bricklayers on scaffolds. There is no one else in the world that can do what he does and he has even put up an award of money to anyone who can beat any of his records. John was once at a big event where the world's strongest man at the time was appearing. He was doing some fantastic feats of strength and getting a lot of applause. When it was John's turn to balance bricks on his head and set a new world record, it brought the house down and he was the star of the event. Even world's strongest men from the World's Strongest Man Organization have never taken on the challenge of this amazing feat of strength John has for balancing a total weight of around 400 lb. on his head. Not only does he balance these things, he also walks with them.

John has appeared on television shows all over the world, including: *The Tonight Show with Jay Leno, Wow! The Most Awesome Acts on Earth, Guinness World Records™ Live! The Top 100 Records of All Time*, prime time, and *Live with Regis and Kathy Lee*, to name just a few. He has also raised several hundreds of thousands of pounds for many charities over the years and will continue to do so.

Girl in Oil Drum on Fire
John Evans.

Girl on Bed
John Evans.

House Bricks
101 (416 lb.) John Evans.

Largest Item of Volume Balanced on Head
Size: 10 feet wide by 5 feet 5 inches high. Using 15 Gorilla Tubs. John Evans.

Loaves of Bread
300 (378 lb.) John Evans.

Milk Crates
98 (347 lb.) John Evans.

Motorcycle
345 lb. John Evans.

Oil Drums
6. John Evans.

Patio Tables (7)
12 feet 9 inches high. John Evans.

People
92 in 1 hour (total weight of 11,420 lb.) John Evans.

Peter Dowdeswell Drinking Yard of Ale on Bed of Nails
John Evans.

Pints of Beer
236. John Evans.

Quad Bike
363 lb. John Evans.

Soccer Balls
548: 335 lb. John Evans.

While Steve Martin Juggled 3 Flaming Clubs
2 minutes, 19 seconds. John Evans.

Stone Fireplace
396 lb. John Evans.

Stones
365 lb. John Evans.

Tall Refrigerator / Freezer
297 lb. John Evans.

Tires
10. John Evans.

Two Girls on Bikes
382 lb. John Evans.

Washing Machines (2)
363 lb. John Evans.

Water Kegs
13. John Evans.

Wooden Beer Barrels (3)
John Evans.

Helicopter Landing

Supporting 1,188 lb. for 35 seconds. Franz Muellner.

Thienna Ho

41-year-old female.
Married with no children.
Scientific nutritionist, leading skin care author of
Unlocking the Mystery of Skin Color.
Web: www.thienna.com
E-mail: thienna@thienna.com

World's Greatest Super Sumo Squatter:
Most squats in 1 hour: 5,135

Thienna Ho, Ph.D., was born in Saigon, Vietnam, in 1968, just three months after Vietcong forces attacked the city during the infamous Tet Offensive. Eleven years later, Thienna and her family fled communist Vietnam in a 50-foot wooden boat. During the harrowing ocean voyage to Indonesia, Thienna's vessel was attacked five times by pirates. Less than a year later, Thienna and her family immigrated to the United States and settled in San Francisco.

Thienna was first introduced to the Sumo Squat by her father when she was 5 years old! She started practicing the Sumo Squat in her late 20's. Sumo Squats work every major muscle group in the body. Specifically, they help to strengthen problem areas, such as the inner and outer thighs, while working the whole upper body. It provides a vigorous cardiovascular workout and improves flexibility of the legs. Thienna is thrilled about having achieved this world record, not only for personal satisfaction, but she also wants to raise awareness of the benefits associated with Sumo Squat exercises for women. Squat exercises are typically associated with men. Her hope is that women will embrace this exercise, as it targets many common problem areas typically concerning women.

Highland Games

First Female
Cynthia Morrison aka "Cindini." In 1994, Cynthia became the first female to compete professionally in Scotland's Highland Games—an intense athletics competition that includes such events as the caber toss and hammer throw.

Hot Water Bottle Bursting

Fastest
35.6 seconds. Set on October 26, 2003, the record for bursting a British standard hot water bottle is 35.6 seconds, by Fred Burton at The Winking Man night club, near Leek, Staffordshire, United Kingdom. BOAR

LADY JAILBREAKER, STRONG WOMAN, AND PRE-EMINENT FEMALE ESCAPOLOGIST, CYNTHIA MORRISON, AKA, "THE GREAT CINDINI," IS THE HOLDER OF NUMEROUS WORLD RECORDS INCLUDING THE FASTEST HANDCUFF ESCAPES ON BOTH LAND AND UNDERWATER!

cartoon by Sean Hopkins

Human Floor

Weight on Body
Most: 3,126 lb. Pete Tino aka "The Human Floor." 24 women weighing 3,126 lb. were maintained for 10 seconds, while lying supine.

Lifting

Most Weight with Eyelashes
Three 50-ounce bottles of Coca-Cola from string attached to his eyelashes. Ashok Verma. ASIA BOOK OF RECORDS

Most Weight with Teeth
110 lb. Wasantha Kumara. ASIA BOOK OF RECORDS

Log Carrying

Fastest
100 logs weighing 55 lb. each, moved one at a time, 32.8 feet (10 m): 16 minutes, 42.37 seconds. Fred Burton. BOAR

Medicine Ball

Chest Pass
1 minute: 112. Dave Robinson and Paul Norris.

2 minutes: 163. Mark Gear and Paul Norris.

5 minutes: 524. Paul Norris and Dave Robinson.

Hula Pass
1 minute: 40 passes. Vanessa Relph.

Most Snatches with a 8 kg Double Grip Medicine Ball
Time: 10 minutes. 355. Paul Woodland.

Sit-up Pass
154. Dave Robinson and Paul Norris.

Steve Mills
OF THE Dazzling Mills Family

50-year-old male.
Marion, OH, USA.
Married with two children.
Entertainer, professional circus actor, juggler.
Web: www.dazzlingmills.com
E-mail: steve@dazzlingmills.com

2 World Records:

Most weight ridden on 3 person high unicycle:
495 lb.

Golf tee balanced on nose with golf ball:
38 seconds

Steve Mills has won 12 national and international awards with his family, as well as 2 world records. He also appeared on 9 national television performances as he and his family are world renowned jugglers. The Dazzling Mills Family has performed on cruise ships, with the Harlem Globetrotters, and at many schools and fairs.

Steve started unicycling at 14 years old and shortly thereafter, learned to juggle from famous mathematician, Ron Graham. Three years later, at the age of 17, he won the first of 3 international juggling championships. Steve then married his wife Carol, the 6-time national unicycling champion, and eight years later they had their first child, Michelle. Michelle performed for the first time at 3 days old! And she has not missed more than a handful of shows since. Steve's son Tony was born 5 years later, in 1991. Tony is an incredible performer and started unicycling at 5 years old! Steve is the inventor of the world famous juggling pattern called Mills' Mess.

Standing Chest Press
10 lb.: 1 minute: 153. Paddy Doyle.

10 lb.: 5 minutes: 477. Paddy Doyle.

Standing Torso Twist
10 lb.: 1 minute: 90. Paddy Doyle.

10 lb.: 10 minutes: 684. Paddy Doyle.

10 lb.: 15 minutes: 1,042. Paddy Doyle.

Throw
37.7 feet (11.5 m). Jermaine Bernard.

Torso Twist Pass
1 minute: 112. Richard Talbot and Vanessa Relph.

2 minutes: 142. Richard Talbot and Vanessa Relph.

5 minutes: 352. Richard Talbot and Vanessa Relph.

Nail Hammering

Fastest with Hand
116. On October 2, 1999, Chu-Tan Cuong of Germany, used his hand to drive 116 nails into a wooden board in a time of 11 minutes. BOAR

Playing Cards

Most Torn
135. On March 15, 1930, Milo Barus (real name, Emil Bahr) of Germany, tore a deck of 135 playing cards in Paris at a world's strongest man contest. BOAR

Railway Carriage Pulling

With Teeth
Weight: 20.5 tons. Distance: 656 feet (200 m). Sekhar Ranawat. ASIA BOOK OF RECORDS

Rickshaw Pulling

Furthest Distance
1,351.5 miles. Covering a distance of 1,351.5 miles (2,175 km) in 50 days, Sitdek Ahmad Ali of Malaysia, hand-pulled a rickshaw from October 1 to November 19, 2000, traveling a distance between 31 and 50 miles (50–80 km) per day. BOAR

Rolls Royce Pull

Greatest Distance by a Female
52 feet. Cynthia Morrison. Performed with the use of a chest harness.

Skipping

Longest Duration with a 48 lb. Chain
1 hour, 30 minutes. Walter Cornelius.

Spike Bending

Most in 1 Hour
368. George Christen of Luxembourg, bent 368 iron nails (210 mm long with a diameter of 7 mm) into a "U" or "V" shape within a time of one hour. BOAR

Step-ups

On 15-inch Box
40 lb. backpack: 1 hour: 1,619. Paddy Doyle.

56 lb. backpack: 1 hour: 1,228. Stuart Barr.

Franz Muellner
"The Grizzly"

37-year-old male.
Salzburg, Austria.
Married with two children.
Professional extreme sportsman.
Web: www.muellner-franz.at
E-mail: info@muellner-franz.at

4 World Records as "The Grizzly:"

Helicopter landing supporting 1,188 lb.:
35 seconds

Longest wheelie with a Ferrari Modena:
13.45 seconds

Pulling a 78-ton Airbus 321:
20 meters in 10 seconds

Truck pulling: 59.8 tons for 20 meters

Franz Muellner started extreme sports at the age of 18, competing in events such as marathons and triathlons (Ironman distance). While with the federal army, he did parachuting and was trained to be a ranger. Franz was always looking for more extremes. He became a strongman because he wanted to know how strong a man could be. After attaining several honors (the strongest man of Austria for 3 years, a worldwide ranking of 15, and a 2-time European champion) Franz had the impulse to do more crazy and extreme things—and now he is what he is.

He's appeared on world record shows around the world, including: CCTV in Beijing, TV Azteka Mexico, RAI it, Eurosport, several television stations in Germany and Austria, such as ORF, ZDF, DAS ERSTE, PRO 7, *RTL Guinness World Record™ Show*, DSF, 3sat, VOX, SAT 1, Salzburg TV, ATV, plus his world records have appeared three times in the *Guinness Book of World Records* and now in *Ripley's*. Franz's greatest accomplishment is creating and finally setting the world records in helicopter landing and holding back a race car at the wheelie. He is currently creating and testing new crazy ideas—for example, turning the giant Ferris wheel in Prater, Vienna by hand. Says Franz, "I'm always living at the limit and the extreme side of life."

Sumo Squats

Most in 1 Hour
5,135. Thienna Ho.

Tractor Pulling

Fastest Mile with Team
On March 28, 1998, three men from North Carolina, USA, set a world record by pulling a 27,000 lb. (12,247.2 kg) tractor-trailer a distance of 1 mile in the record time of 95 minutes, 16 seconds. Kirk Nobles, John Brookfield, and Steve Jeck completed the mile-long feat in the presence of Fairmont, North Carolina Mayor Pro Tem, Charles Kemp, who doubled as official timekeeper. BOAR

Train Pulling

Furthest
220 yards. George Christen of Luxembourg, pulled a 20.5-ton railway carriage with his teeth for a distance of 220 yards (200 m), on August 18, 1985. BOAR

Furthest on Hands with Teeth
4.59 feet. Jan Knotek of the Czech Republic, pulled a railway carriage weighing 15 tons a distance of 4.59 feet while walking on his hands, pulling the rope using only his teeth. BOAR

Truck Pulling

Heaviest
59.8 tons: 20 meters. Franz Muellner.

Unicycle

Most Weight
497 lb. On February 3, 2007, Steve Mills of The

Dazzling Mills Family, cycled a 20-inch unicycle 28 feet 2 inches whilst his daughter, Michelle, sat on his shoulders and her brother, Anthony, sat on her shoulders. (Total weight: 497 lb.)

Rope Skips
51. Jem Famous.

Watermelon Smashing

Broken with Head
1 minute: 62. Abid Khan. ASIA BOOK OF RECORDS

Weight Lifting

Most with Tongue
26.4 lb. (12 kg). June 2007. Thomas Blackthorne.

Triceps Lift
1 hour: 2,393.6 lb. (1,088 kg). Stuart Burrell.

With 1 Finger
252 lb. For World Cup. Fred Burton.

With Teeth
112 lb. Fred Burton.

1 Hour
149,220 lb. Paddy Doyle.

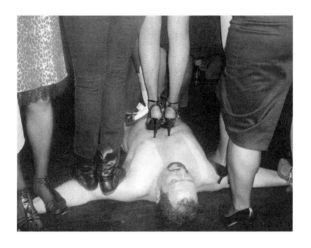

Pete Tino
"The Human Floor"

45-year-old male.
Taunton, MA, USA.
Sideshow performer.
Web: www.myspace.com/thehumanfloor
E-mail: Lifter1121@comcast.net

World Record:
24 women standing on body while lying supine:
total weight of 3,126 lb.

Pete Tino aka "The Human Floor," is one of the strangest and most amazing performers you will ever see. In addition to his acts as a strong-man and pain-resister, Pete performs The Bed of Nails, where he will lay down on a bed of very long, very sharp nails, while a woman in bondage gear jump ropes atop his chest. He also performs the Staple Gun act, where people take a carpenter's staple gun and staple dollar bills onto his body, including the face and forehead. Pete presents the audience with the ultimate routine of audience participation. His act is one of the most incredible and unforgettable things you will ever see, one that has placed him on stages around the world. Have you ever seen two dozen women in high heels standing atop a man, including his arms, thighs, and face?

Pete is a gentle giant of a man whose threshold for pain must be seen to be believed. He has been amazing audiences throughout the country for years. On Hank's Dairy Barn in Plainfield, Connecticut, he set a world record when 24 women with a combined weight of 3,126 lb. used him like a bus stop. Pete has performed on *The Tyra Banks Show*, *HBO Late Night with Katie Morgan*, the sideshow at the Opie & Anthony Virus Tour, and Vicious Vaudeville.

Chapter 2

Pastimes and the Arts

How many times have we heard the expression, "Haven't you anything better to do?" or perhaps, "He's got too much free time on his hands." So what do people do when they've got too much time on their hands *and* nothing better to do with it? How about sitting in a bath of beans or throwing custard pies or stuffing ferrets down their pant legs or running around an old jail house tied up in leg-irons?

Some would say, "They're crazy." Others would say, "Now, that's cool. Why didn't I think of that?" Well, regardless of what you would say, just be sure you've got plenty of free time on your hands, hope that not too many people are watching, and you've got a camera on hand to prove it.

Abseiling

Oldest
95 years, 5 days. Doris Long.

Adoptee

Oldest
78 years of age. Buddy Pierce.

After Dinner Speaking

Longest Duration
32 hours, 25 minutes. Donald "Spiderman" Thomas.

Animal Impersonator

Most
100. Russell Davies.

Quickest in 1 Minute
30. Russell Davies.

Band

Most Countries Traveled
89. Liquid Blue has performed in 89 countries throughout the world between 1997 and 2006. (Note: the next most traveled band is The Rolling Stones, with 42 countries.) Record submitted March 11, 2007.

Bass Guitar

Fastest Percussive Notes per Second
36. Jayen Varma.

Bath

Longest in Baked Beans
100 hours. The longest recorded time for a sit-in in

Scott Baker

The World's Greatest Sideshow Talker, The Bally Master, known in the Sideshow World as "The Twisted Shockmeister"

Web: Coney Island, USA
E-mail: geekcircus@yahoo.com

World Record:
Performed 150 back-to-back sideshow ballys while performing Human Blockhead— ramming an 8-inch screwdriver into his skull— for 6 hours, 43 minutes on September 13, 2009.

Scott Baker starred on Broadway for 12 years in the legendary *Oh! Calcutta*, performed the leading role in Las Vegas in *Love Potion Number Ten* with the Coasters, the Drifters and the Platters, and broke attendance records at La Mama in New York with his show *Geek Circus: The Twisted Shockfest.* This wild show took him to the Edinburgh Fringe Festival, where he was awarded "People's Choice" by the *Manchester Guardian*, and was the first American ever invited to perform with Edinburgh's notorious late-night cabaret, *The Establishment*. On American television, Scott has performed comedy sketches on *The Late Show with David Letterman, Late Night with Conan O'Brien, The Chris Rock Show, Chappelle's Show, MTV Oddville*, many late night comedies seen on Cinemax, Showtime and HBO, and has starred in many commercials.

In addition to being a performer, Scott is a playwright, whose *Booth: An American Vaudeville*, will be seen in New York next season. His homage to old-time burlesque, *Scott Baker's Coney Island Babies*, the naughty, bawdy, baggy-pants laugh riot, can be seen Off-Broadway in 2010.

For 14 seasons, Scott has performed with Coney Island Sideshows by the Seashore—the last traditional ten-in-one live sideshow in the world—where he has performed all of the acts on the inside show and brought thousands of people in with his skills as "outside talker," making him the number-one sideshow talker in history. He is the subject of Gary Beeber's movie *Bally Master*, which won 8 "Best Documentary" awards at film festivals around the world. His figure-skating act, *Magic on Ice*, at the Coney Island Ice Theatre, is an event for which he was also the emcee, combining two of his passions, ice skating and magic.

a bath of cold baked beans is 100 hours, by Barry "Captain Beany" Kirk of Port Talbot, West Glamorgan, United Kingdom. Barry's "Bean-a-thon" was staged at the Aberavon Hotel from September 11 to 15, 1986. BOAR

Longest in Custard
168 hours. Former Army PT Instructor Bill Hammond, 52, of Pickering, North Yorkshire, United Kingdom, set a new world record in June 1988 sitting in a bath full of custard for 168 hours in a shop window. BOAR

Longest in Milk
48 hours. 25-year-old Doris Bray of Sydney, Australia, sat in a bath of milk for 48 hours in May 1989. BOAR

Longest in Porridge
122 hours, 30 minutes. Starting on April 1, 1988, landlord Philip Heard set a new world record of 122 hours, 30 minutes, sitting in a bath of cold porridge at his pub in Hanam, Bristol, United Kingdom. BOAR

Longest in Spaghetti
360 hours. Rob Gordon, 24, of Shrewsbury, Shropshire, United Kingdom, sat in a bath of spaghetti for 360 hours, starting on September 21 and finishing on October 6,1984. The bath was mounted on a wheeled trolley so that Rob could be pushed around the streets of Shrewsbury and also continue his disc jockey duties in the evenings. BOAR

Pushing for 10 Miles
1 hour, 41 minutes. The record for pushing a bath (mounted on wheels) for 10 miles, stands at 1 hour,

41 minutes, 44.38 seconds, by three members of Yateley Hockey Club: Rowan Atkins, Alan Hancock, and Giles Hancock (passenger). Set on July 11, 1987. BOAR

Beard

Longest
6 feet. Shamsher Singh. Last measured on August 18, 1997. ASIA BOOK OF RECORDS

Bed of Glass

Longest Lying
76 hours. The longest time recorded for lying on a bed of broken glass is 76 hours. Tom Miller of Australia, carried out this record between April 1 and 4, 1989. BOAR

Most Weight
938 lb. Cynthia Morrison aka "The Great Cindini" laid upon broken glass (without protection) and had a plywood board on her chest, upon which people stood for 10.87 seconds. February 1, 2007.

Supine Rotations
22: 33 minutes, 24 seconds. Reed McClintock. While lying supine upon a bed of broken glass, Reed made twenty-two 360° rotations in 33 minutes, 24 seconds. His back remained in contact with the glass at all times.

Walking on Glass
Time: 1 hour. Distance: 0.67 miles (1,060 m). Nigel Jardine.

Longest distance: 18.6 miles (30 km). Time: 27.5 hours. Nigel Jardine.

Weight
2,229.95 lb. Rainer Schröder of Germany. The greatest weight held whilst lying on a bed of glass is 2,229.95 lb. (1,011.5 kg). April 2002. BOAR

Bed of Glass and Bed of Nails

Most Weight Held
502 lb. Cynthia Morrison aka "The Great Cindini," laid upon a bed of broken glass with a bed of nails on her torso, upon which 2 men stood, weighing a total 502 lb.

Bed of Nails

Iron Maiden
2 beds of nails. Most weight: 1,888 lb. On May 5, 1998, John Ferraro aka "Gino Martino," sandwiched himself between two 24 x 48 inch beds of nails (162 4-inch nails, 2 inches apart) upon which 4 humans stood, weighing a total of 1,888 lb. (858 kg), for 10 seconds.

Lying
292 hours. Visheswar Sharma. ASIA BOOK OF RECORDS

Weight
3,638 lb. On BBC Television's *Late, Late Breakfast Show* on December 10, 1983, John Kassar lay on a bed of unblunted, 6-inch nails. A wooden board was placed on his chest and 29 girls climbed onto it. The total weight pressing down on John's body was 3,638 lb. (1,650 kg). Although his body was marked, the sharp nails did not penetrate the skin. BOAR

Heaviest Weight Broken (Solid Ice Block)
1,224 lb. Roy Maloy. Using sledgehammers, six men

smashed a 1,224 lb. solid block of ice placed upon Roy whilst laying supine on a bed of nails.

Bed of Swords

Lying

Longest: 36 hours, 10 minutes. The longest recorded time for laying across the sharpened blades of four military swords is 36 hours, 10 minutes, by Tom Miller of Fremantle of Australia, September 17–18, 1988. BOAR

Beermat Stuffing

In Mouth

77. The greatest number of standard beermats ever stuffed into a mouth and held by the teeth is 77, by David Armitage at the Goat Inn, Steeton, Yorkshire, United Kingdom, on April 1, 1990. BOAR

Beermat Tower

Tallest

48 feet. Using 76,320 beermats, a team of six, all members of a club of brewery collectibles collectors, built a tower of beermats measuring 48 feet (14.66 m) in height. This record was achieved by Stephan Carstensen, Burkhard Ohrt, Sascha Janssen, Mark Hirt, Bernd Jensen, and Kai Suckow of Germany, within six days of starting, in April 1994. BOAR

Bell Ringing

Longest Peal Rung

50,400. David Pipe, Andrew Tibbetts, and Philip Earis of the United Kingdom, have broken the 41-year-old world record for the longest peal ever rung. Their new record for the greatest number of changes in a peal

Madeline Barnes

10-year-old female.
Boston, MA, USA.
Student.
E-mail: ebarnes59@aol.com

World Record:
Smallest origami fortune teller

Madeline Barnes is 10 years old, in the fourth grade, and lives in Massachusetts. She has a younger sister, a mom, and a dad. She also has many pets at home, and the pet she has bonded with the most is her Labrador retriever. Madeline takes karate lessons and has been riding horses for six years. She also plays the drums, enjoys gymnastics, and loves to cook, sketch, paint, and write poetry. Madeline hopes to be an author someday.

She has been interested in setting a world record since she was in kindergarten. Madeline saw a world record book in the library and was fascinated by all the things people could do. She decided that she would try to break a world record because she wanted to do something very few people have done. Madeline chose the Japanese fortune-teller because it is a beautiful piece of origami. A friend of hers taught her how to make one at school and she found it fun and easy. Each time she made one, she tried to make it smaller. Soon, Madeline managed to make it a half inch! She was excited to find out that it was the smallest origami fortune-teller in the world.

is 50,400. The attempt lasted for 17 hours, 6 minutes and took place October 2, 2004, at the Ancient Society of College Youths in Coventry. BOAR

Bharatanatyam

Arangetram: Youngest Dancer
8 years of age. Miss Priyanshi Parikh (daughter of Deepali and Pragnesh Parikh) performed the difficult Indian religious dance on May 16, 2006.

Bible (New Testament)

Largest Hand Written
Sunil Joseph. This handwritten Bible has the following properties: 1) one verse per page; 2) heaviest at 143 lb.; 3) thickest at 3 feet 7 inches; 4) written in 123 days; 5) maximum number of pages at 16,000; 6) written on butter paper; 7) mirror image; 8) handwritten; and 9) lies vertical.

Team
Fastest: 15 minutes, 36 seconds. A group of 7,798 Royal Rangers Boy Scouts wrote down the entire Bible by hand in 15 minutes, 36 seconds on August 1, 2005 in Neufrankenroda, Germany. Their sheets of paper were assembled to a complete handwritten Bible weighing 70.4 lb. BOAR

Blood Donation

Most Gallons
114. Philip Whitford of Casselberry, FL, has donated 114 gallons (912 pints) of blood as of November 12, 2006. Record validated and submitted by Florida's Blood Centers, USA.

Body in Box

Smallest Box
60 x 30 x 40 centimeters is entered and closed. Wu Xizi. Venue: Nanjing, in eastern China on May 22, 2006. ASIA BOOK OF RECORDS

Body Piercings

Most
500 with 3,420 tattoos. Elaine Davidson.

Book Signing

Deepest
12,465 feet below sea level. Fran Capo of Putnam Valley, NY, USA, performed the deepest book signing in a submersible at the wreck site of the Titanic on July 10, 2005. She signed an edition of *Ripley's Planet Eccentric, Adrenaline Adventures,* and *Almost a Wise Guy.* The site is 380 miles southeast of Newfoundland in the North Atlantic Ocean.

Highest
19,340 feet on Mt. Kilimanjaro. Fran Capo of Putnam Valley, NY, USA, performed the highest book signing at the top of the world (Mt. Kilimanjaro, 19,340 feet) on July 10, 2004. The books were *Adrenaline Adventures* and *Almost a Wise Guy.* They were signed in weather conditions of -15°F and 45 mph winds.

Burn (full-body without oxygen)

Longest
7 minutes, 44 seconds. On November 12, 2006, Mark Mosier of Eldersburg, MD, USA, performed a full-body burn for an incredible 7 minutes, 44 seconds without the aid of oxygen. This remarkably

Ricardo Bellino
The World's Fastest Deal-maker

43-year-old male.
Key Biscayne, FL, USA.
Married with two children.
Entrepreneur and author.
Web: www.goldbell.com.br
E-mail: ricardo@goldbell.com.br

World Record:
Fastest multimillion dollar business deal:
3 minutes

Ricardo Bellino was born in Sao Paulo, Brazil, and as a young college student, devised a plan to bring Elite Models Agency and The Look of the Year, the most famous modeling contest in the world, to Brazil. Ricardo is the founder and former CEO of Trump Realty Brazil, an enterprise that created the largest golf complex in Latin America, Villa Trump, the result of his famous "3 minute" meeting with Donald Trump.

Ricardo has authored four business books focusing on the power of ideas and sales techniques. In particular, his most famous book, *You Have 3 Minutes!*, is now printed in several languages and is a number-one seller around the world. Sometime after his big deal with Donald Trump and the success of his books, Ricardo pursued the possibility of his achievement becoming a world record. It was accepted by Record Holders Republic and was the focus of a business banquet in his honor held by the Brazilian Entrepreneur's Association.

dangerous feat was performed with over one year of planning by the team of Mark Mosier, Jeff Wilhelm, and Mick Kipp.

Burp

Alphabet
19 seconds. Will Jones.

Loudest
118.1 decibels. Paul Hunn.

Candle Blowing

1 Breath
144. Alastair Galpin of New Zealand, blew out 144 candles with a single breath in Mt. Albert, Auckland, New Zealand on February 19, 2005. BOAR

Car Washing

Duration
72 hours: 188 cars. Full-time car washer Otto Dettl of Austria, washed 188 cars in 72 hours, setting a new endurance world record in 1985. BOAR

Card Fan

Most
326. Ralf Laue.

Cave Dwelling

Longest
463 days. The longest period of time that a human has voluntarily remained totally isolated from the rest of civilization is 463 days, by the self-styled troglodyte Milutin Veljkovic of Yugoslavia. For scientific purposes, he stood in the Samar cave from June 24, 1969 to September 30, 1970. BOAR

Celebrity Phone Messages

246: 3.7 years (1,344 days): Jason Antone. Jason received 246 congratulatory phone calls and messages from show business celebrities for his TV show, the *JROCK SHOW*, in West Bloomfield, MI. Jason received his first phone call on February 1, 2006 and, as of October 8, 2009, is still receiving celebrity calls.

Chalk (interlocking links)

Most

15 links made from chalk to a length of 75 millimeters. Satish Kumar. Venue: Ravindra Bharat Auditorium, India on August 19, 2007.

Chiropractic Care

Most Patients

2 days: 21,545. On April 4th and 5th, 2008, Rock-MeTV host, Fran Capo and cameraman, Jeff Cobelli, volunteered to document the humanitarian world record efforts of *Chiromission.org* in the Dominican Republic. Armed with a group of 28 chiropractors, 31 chiropractic assistants, and 5 volunteers, which included the host and cameraman, 21,545 patients (ages 6 months to 98 years old) were cared for over a two-day period throughout the Dominican Republic and Haiti. Chiromission, which was founded by J.C. Doornick, Todd Herold, and Pete Morgan, broke into teams and went into orphanages, jails, churches, schools, and village streets to volunteer their services.

Cigarettes

Orally Extinguished, Chewed, and Expelled

200 (1 carton): 6 minutes, 3.7 seconds. Richie Magic.

Jonathon Bryce

28-year-old male.
Bloomington, MN, USA.
Daredevil escape artist and illusionist.
Web: www.jonathonbryce.com
www.myspace.com/jonathonbryce

World Record:
24 different escapes in 24 hours in 24 different
cities in the state of Minnesota on
October 27, 2007

Jonathon Bryce has been privileged to study his craft under the watchful eyes of America's most respected magicians and escape artists. Performers like Rudy Coby, Jeff McBride, Andre Kole, Al Schnider, and John Bushy have had a direct influence in Jonathon's career and have not only given him the motivation to invent illusions and escapes, but to continue to find ways to perform them in unique ways, something nobody else does!

Jonathon's energetic blend of illusions and escapes have been seen by audiences around the world, including many regional and national politicians, musical legends like Bono, Marilyn Manson, Blondie, and Pat Boone, and the Royal Family of Monaco along with 3,000 of their best friends. He's performed at the Edinburgh Fringe Festival, the Singapore Comedy Festival, county fairs, city celebrations, regional theaters, schools, hospitals, and other similar institutions. Jonathon's work has been seen on BBC, ORF television in Austria, *The Today Show* on NBC, *Good Morning America*, TNN's *Crook & Chase*, and *The Early Show* on CBS. He gladly lives like a king one week and a pauper the next as he continues to invent, study, and amaze audiences with the ancient art of illusions and escapes.

Orally Extinguished, Chewed, and Expelled (1 at a time)
20: 29.0 seconds. Richie Magic (The Human Ashtray).

Cocktail Mixing

Longest
72 hours, 5 minutes. In 2000, at the 5th Saxonia Record Festival held in Germany, Christian Vögel of Bregenz, Austria, mixed cocktails non-stop for 72 hours, 5 minutes. BOAR

Comedy (stand-up)

Most Punch Lines in 8 Minutes
73. On June 3, 2006, stand-up comedian Paul Nardizzi delivered 73 distinct punch lines in 8 minutes, each causing an audible laugh by the audience at a performance at the Crown Plaza Hotel, Pittsfield, MA, USA.

Computer Game Playing

Longest
166 hours. The record for playing a computer game was broken when Jürgen Kopmann of Germany, played the computer game "Fate: Gates of Dawn" for 166 hours in 1991. BOAR

Continuous Live Performance of a Piece of Music

168 hours: The All Stars Collective. The All Stars Collective played "The Pizza Express Never Ending Song" non-stop, for 24 hours a day, 7 consecutive days.

Counting

1 Breath
1 through 400. Paramjit Singh. Paramjit counted the

consecutive numbers 1 through 400 in 45 seconds with just one breath.

Court Case

Civil
Longest unresolved: 13,556 days (37 years, 1 month, 11 days). James L. Martin. Proceedings of Martin v. Sample began 12/14/1972 and remains unresolved as of 1/24/2010.

Crawling

Furthest
35 miles (56.62 km). Suresh Joachim.

Crickets

Eaten
1 minute: 37. Don "Inferno" Williamson.

Custard Pies

Most Thrown
2,350 in 2 minutes, 30 seconds. CIRCUS OF HORRORS

Dance Marathon

Longest
100 hours. Suresh Joachim.

Eating

Lightbulbs
Fastest: 50.06 seconds. Todd Robbins.

Lifetime: 4,000 plus. Todd Robbins.

Egg and Spoon Racing

50 Meters
7.9 seconds. Josef Bohman of Czechoslovakia,

John Ferraro
"The Extreme Strongman,
Gino Martino"

33-year-old male.
Boston, MA, USA.
Two daughters, Giavanna and Jenna.
Professional strongman, professional wrestler,
vice president of sales and marketing.
Web: www.ginomartino.com, www.myspace.com/ginomartino
E-mail: gino_martino@hotmail.com

Personal Philosophy:
"It's mind over matter: If you're out of your
mind…it just don't matter!"

5 World Records:
Most concrete blocks broken on head with
bowling ball: 6

Most concrete blocks broken with back: 10

Most concrete blocks broken with head: 4

Most weight in an iron maiden: 1,888 lb.

Thickest concrete block broken on head:
8 inches

John Ferraro is the powerhouse performer known as The Extreme Strongman: the man with the hardest skull in the world. John does demonstrations featuring death-defying feats of mental and physical toughness, not to mention explosive power. He performs a wide array of incredible strength feats, including the use of sledgehammers, jackhammers, bowling balls, beds of barbed wire, and beds of nails. John is a certified master of Iron Chi Kung, an elite level cement breaking champion, and power lifter who has benched-pressed in excess 550 lb. and curled with dumbbells over 140 lb. each.

John has performed insane exhibitions in front of crowds throughout the USA and Canada. He appeared on CMT'S *Country Fried Home Videos* having a cement block jackhammered on his iron skull. John is not only a world record setter and breaker, but a professional wrestler with 12 years of experience. He was internationally ranked as a professional wrestler in 2001, 2002, 2003, and 2005. John prefers wrestling his opponents in hard-core events that involve barbed wire, fire, thumbtacks, and broken glass. His favorite professional wrestling move is a skull-shattering head butt. Would you expect anything different?

established the record for egg and spoon racing for a distance of 50 meters in a time of 7.9 seconds. BOAR

Held in Hand
100 meters. Fastest: 19 seconds. The fastest egg and spoon racer is Jan Trenik of the Czech Republic. At the Festival of Records in Pelhrimov, he ran 100 meters in 19.0 seconds on June 22, 1991. BOAR

Held in Mouth
10 miles (16.2 km). Rirí Václavík of the Czech Republic walked a distance of 16.2 kilometers while carrying an egg on a spoon held in his mouth on June 10, 1994 at the Festival of Records in Pelhrimov. BOAR

EX CON-MAN AND SLEIGHT-OF-HAND ARTIST, SIMON LOVELL, HOLDS MULTIPLE CARD HANDLING WORLD RECORDS AS WELL AS HAVING THE LONGEST RUNNING ONE MAN OFF-BROADWAY SHOW IN NYC HISTORY!

artoon by Sean Hopkins

Escalator Ride

Longest
140 miles (225.44 km) up and down. Suresh Joachim.

Escapes

Most
24 hours: 24 cities. Jonathon Bryce of Bloomington, MN, USA performed 24 different escapes in 24 different cities in the state of Minnesota on October 27, 2007.

Eye Protrusion

Distance
11 millimeters beyond her eye sockets. Kim Goel.
ASIA BOOK OF RECORDS

Eyelashes

Longest
2.8 centimeters. Sahebro Rajaram. ASIA BOOK OF RECORDS

Fancy Dress

Largest Gathering
165. John Huggins. Southwold Common, Southwold, Suffolk, United Kingdom.

Ferret Legging

*Longest*5 hours, 26 minutes. The undisputed World Ferret Legging Champion is 78-year-old Reg Mellor (d. 1987) of Barnsley, Yorkshire, United Kingdom. Indeed, Reg claimed to be the originator of this "sport" when, as a boy of 8, he used to keep his hunting ferrets warm and dry by stuffing them down his trousers after a day in the fields. On July 5, 1981, at the Annual Pennine Show in Holmfirth, Yorkshire, Reg broke his own world records by keeping two live ferrets down his trousers for a time of 5 hours, 26 minutes. Reg performed the feat in front of over 5,000 people, and although badly bitten in "all the wrong places," he persevered to the bitter end. BOAR

Fire

Fire Breathing
Most fireballs blown in one minute: 25. Flambeaux (Chris Reilly)

Fire Breathing
Fire balls blown with one mouthful of fuel: 19. Don "Inferno" Williamson.

Fire Breathing (vertical blow)
27 feet. Don "Inferno" Williamson.

Most Torches Extinguished in Hand
1 minute: 47. Don "Inferno" Williamson.

Most Torches Extinguished while Inverted
1 minute: 14. The Great Cindini (Cynthia Morrison)

Most Blow Transfers
15 seconds: 37. Tyler Fyre.

Torches Extinguished in Mouth at One Time
8. Don "Inferno" Williamson.

Torches Extinguished in Mouth One at a Time
1 minute: 61. Jens Palmkivst. BOAR.

Torch in Mouth
Longest duration: 55.53 seconds. Flambeaux (Chris Reilly).

Foot Balancing

On One
Longest: 76 hours, 40 minutes. Suresh Joachim.

Frying Pan Throwing

Distance
156 feet. Jürgen Schult of Germany, threw a frying pan a record distance of 47.60 meters at a sports meeting in Schwerin, Germany. BOAR

Glass Box

Scorpions
Longest time in box: 32 days with 3,400 scorpions. Knchana Ketkeaw. ASIA BOOK OF RECORDS

Gloves

Worn
7. Alastair Galpin. Venue: The Old Homestead, Point Chevalier, Auckland, New Zealand in May 2006.

Goldfish

Swallowed
1 minute: 30. Ray "Buster" Brabant.

Golf Ball Holding

22. Zdenek Bradac. BOAR

Jamie Alisha Jackson
The World's Fastest Bouquet Catcher

Draper, UT, USA.
Not married…yet.
Professional bouquet catcher, personal trainer,
bachelor's degree in exercise and sport science:
ACE & CSCS certifications.
E-mail: peachhead11@yahoo.com

World Record:
A smashing record of 38 clean and caught
wedding bouquets!

Jamie Jackson started catching wedding
bouquets at the age of 18 and has been catching
bouquets ever since! Her record of 35 has been
true and blue as the sky itself! No, she's not a
wedding crasher…she has personally been
invited to every one of these weddings and
has even knocked out some little girls in the
process—you see she has no mercy—when

it's game time watch out! Seriously! She never expected to catch so many, but practice has made perfect and she's been doing pretty darn good!

It was always the running joke that Jamie would say to everyone, "I'm going to be in the *Guinness Book of World Records* for catching the most wedding bouquets!" —wink wink, nudge nudge. Well, guess what? Jamie came to find out she is being published in something even better! She is also published in the *Skousen Book of More Amazing Mormon Records.* The technique she uses involves positioning herself in the front of the pack and keeping her eye on the prize! And, of course, humility—the moment she starts getting a little cocky, she comes out empty-handed. Jamie's achievement and legacy will continue until the day she says, "I do!"

Grape Catching

Most

30 minutes: 1,203. The most grapes thrown over a distance of 15 feet and caught in the mouth in 3 minutes is 116, by Steve "The Grape Guy" Spalding of the USA. It was performed in Sydney, Australia on November 16, 2006. On the same occasion, Steve broke the record for 30 minutes, catching 1,203 grapes during this time. BOAR

Mouth

Height: 30 feet. The greatest height from which a grape has been dropped from a moving aircraft (in this case a balloon) and caught in the mouth is 30 feet (9.15 m) by Peter Tilney (dropper) and Tony Gough (catcher) on July 25, 1985. BOAR

Solo

Distance: 39 feet 6 inches. The solo grape catching record belongs to Camilo Antonio Mendez of the United Kingdom. He caught a grape in his mouth thrown a distance of 39 feet 6 inches. BOAR

Gum Wrapper Chain

Longest

1,076,656. Gary Duschl of Virginia Beach, Virginia, USA, holds the record for the longest gum wrapper chain in the world. Gary started the chain on March 11, 1965. Forty years later, on March 11, 2005, the chain contained 1,076,656 gum wrappers and had a length of 46,053 feet (14,046 m). It would take 3 hours to walk the chain's length or nearly 9 minutes by car, traveling at a speed of 60 mph (100 km/h). BOAR

Hair

Ear
Longest: 13.3 centimeters. Radhakant Bajpai. ASIA BOOK OF RECORDS

Longest
18 feet 5.54 inches. Last measured on May 8, 2004. Xie Qiuping of China. ASIA BOOK OF RECORDS

Hand Clapping

1 Hand
1 minute: 354. Amit Shukla.

5 minutes: 1,500. Navnet Singh.

1 Hour
14,200. Paramjit Singh. Paramjit performed this task with a distance of 2 feet between hands for each clap. The claps were audible for between 80 and 100 feet.

Loudest
110.44 decibels. Alastair Galpin.

Handshake

Longest
9 hours. Alastair Galpin with Jesse Van Keken.

Handcuffing

Most People Handcuffed Together at One Time
305. Organized by PC Dave O'Grady at the Hendon Police Training Centre in North London on January 18, 2007.

Heart Bypass Operations

3: Shane Taylor. In a 10-year period from 1997 to

2007, Shane Taylor underwent 3 bypass operations using 11 bypass grafts.

Honey Bees

Body Covered
24 hours: 60,000 bees. C. Jeykumar. ASIA BOOK OF RECORDS

Human Blockhead

Performed Simultaneously
20. Tyler Fyre and Thrill Kill Jill, organizers. Colonel Hunsley, Nicole Gerlach, Gerard Wyatt, Professor Fountain, Professor Sprocket, Gwyd the Unusual, Swami YoMahmi, Mr. Crispy, Harley Newman, Doc Wilson, Tyler Fyre, James Taylor, Thrill Kill Jill, Casey Severn, Screwy Louie, John Shaw, Danny Borneo, James Mundie, Mace Collins, and Johnny Mayhem.

Human Dart Board

Cards Stapled to Body (arm, chest, back, and head)
1 minute: 47. Luke "Kyle Buckett" LeBlanc.

Darts Thrown into Back (½-inch hypodermic needle and syringe)
1 minute: 18. Don "Inferno" Williamson.

Human-Soft Toy Chain

1,258 persons (146 adults, 1,142 children). John Godward (Lord Mayor of Bradford) and the pupils of the Byron School & Bradford Moor School. 1,258 persons formed a human chain, between each was held a soft toy.

Husking Coconuts

With Teeth
5 minutes: 17. K. Ramarao. ASIA BOOK OF RECORDS

Hymn Singing

Duration
40 hours, 17 minutes. Terry Coleman.

Ice Ball

Stacking
539. Gianni Mucignat of Germany, owner of an ice café, holds the world record for stacking ice balls. He stacked 539 ice balls (weighing 17 kg) on one waffle in 1990. BOAR

Individual Chest Hair

Longest
60 millimeters. Alastair Galpin.

Ironing Marathon

MASTER MAGICIAN, RICHIE MAGIC ESTABLISHED THE WORLD RECORD FOR ORALLY EXTINGUISHING A PACK OF CIGARETTES IN 29 SECONDS, A CARTON OF CIGARETTES IN 6 MINUTES 3.7 SECONDS, AND CATCHING 27 SIX-INCH NAILS IN 1 MINUTE!

cartoon by Sean Hopkins

Longest
55 hours, 5 minutes. Suresh Joachim.

Juggling

Standing on Head of Assistant
3 clubs: 72 seconds. James Leonard Martin.

3 fire sticks: 2 minutes, 19 seconds. James Leonard Martin.

Jumping

1 Arm
10 meters: 12.1 seconds. Rodolfo Reyes of Spain, covered a distance of 10 meters while jumping on one hand in a time of 12.1 seconds on June 2, 2006 on a TV show in Munich, Germany. BOAR

Letters

Most Letters Sent by a Dyslexic Person
Approximately 2,500 letters written/sent. Chris Crew.

Most Letters to Editors
7,000. Madhu Agrawal of India, has had published more than 7,000 letters to editors in several Indian newspapers. Her peak year was 2004, when 982 of her letters were published. BOAR

Marriages

Same Person
93. David and Lauren Blair were wed and rewed a total of 93 times.

Matchstick

Most Matches Balanced on a Bottleneck
18,000. Alexander Bendikov. BOAR

Mealworms

Eaten
1 minute: 19. Ray "Buster" Brabant.

Milk Squirting from Eye

Distance
12 feet. This is achieved by sucking milk up the nose.
Praven Kumar Sehrawat of India. ASIA BOOK OF RECORDS

Mirror Writing

Backward Words
318,900. Piyush Dadriwla.

Mobile

Human
21. CIRCUS OF HORRORS

Moon Walking

Marathon
24 hours: 30.60 miles. Suresh Joachim.

Motionless

Longest
35 hours. Akshinthala Seshu Babu stood motionless
in Mahatma Gandhi's posture, with a stick, for the
world record time of 35 hours in 2002. BOAR

Mountain Climbing

United States
48 highest peaks: Shortest time: 23 days, 19 hours,
31 minutes. At 13:01 (GMT) on Tuesday, August
1, 2006, Everest hero Jake Meyer (aged 23) and his

Dan Meyer

51-year-old male.
Hartselle, AL, USA.
Married.
Sword swallower,
Cutting Edge Innertainment Executive Director,
Sword Swallowers Association International (SSAI).
Web: www.cuttingedgeinnertainment.com
E-mail: Dan@swordswallow.com

3 World Records:

Assembled most sword swallowers swallowing swords simultaneously: 19 sword swallowers swallowed 50 swords at once

Most swords swallowed at once by multiple sword swallowers: 52 swords swallowed by 9 sword swallowers

Sword swallowing underwater in a tank of sharks and stingrays: swallowed 30-inch sword with 24-inch blade while submerged 20 feet underwater in a tank of 80 sharks and stingrays

Personal record: Most swords swallowed simultaneously: 8

Hearing in 1998 that there were "less than a dozen sword swallowers left around the world" led Dan Meyer on a quest to locate the surviving sword swallowers while mastering the 4,000-year-old art. After 3 years of research and daily practice, Dan taught himself to swallow swords up to 30 inches long and 8 swords at once while networking the remaining performers into the Sword Swallowers Association International.

As director of SSAI, co-author of a medical study published in the *British Medical Journal* that won the 2007 "Ig Nobel Prize in Medicine" at Harvard, and 3-time Guinness World Record™ holder, best known for swallowing swords underwater in a shark tank for Ripley's Believe It or Not, Dan is recognized as the foremost authority on sword swallowing. Appearances include: *America's Got Talent,* numerous American television broadcasting stations, NPR, BBC, CBC, CTV, NTV Russia, the Discovery Channel, Food Network, *The Today Show, Mancow, Jimmy Kimmel Live!, Rick & Bubba Show, USA Today, Newsweek, National Geographic, Forbes, The New York Times, Scientific American, Nature,* a national tour with Brooks & Dunn's Neon Circus, an international tour with Celtic pop/rock band Ceili Rain, colleges/universities, science/medical centers, churches, corporate and other events around the world.

team of young British adventurers, smashed the existing world record.

Mousetraps

Snapped on Tongue
1 minute: 19. Michael "Gwyd the Unusual" O'Hair.

Mouth Painting

Largest
600 square feet: R. Rajendran. Rajendran, of Puducherry State, India, created his mouth painting with acrylic colors on canvas. It is 30 feet long by 20 feet high, of Mother Teresa, and hangs in India.

Multimillion Dollar Deal

Fastest
3 minutes. On January 28, 2003, Ricardo Bellino met Donald Trump for the very first time at Trump Tower, NY, with the intent of convincing him to build the Villa Trump—an exclusive real estate and golf community in Sao Paulo, Brazil—a half-billion dollar project. Despite being extremely busy and admittedly not in the mood for a new business deal, Mr. Trump reluctantly gave Mr. Bellino exactly 3 minutes to make his presentation. At the end of these 3 minutes, they shook hands and the multi-million dollar deal was sealed on the spot.

Nose Balancing

Golf Ball on Tee
34 seconds. On February 3, 2007, Steve Mills balanced a golf ball atop a 2¾-inch tee on his nose for 34 seconds.

Off-Broadway

Longest Running One-man Show
6 years (and still running). As of January 2010, Simon Lovell's weekly one-man, Off-Broadway sensation, *Simon Lovell's Strange and Unusual Hobbies*, has successfully run for 6 years at the SoHo Playhouse in NYC, USA.

Ongoing Magic Show

Longest Ongoing Annual Magic Show
101 years (1909-2010): Salute to Magic. Eric DeCamps, Dean of Parent Assembly #1, Society of American Magicians.

Onions (mini)

Held in Mouth
16. Dean Gould.

Origami Fortune-teller

Smallest
5 mm x 5 mm. Madeline Barnes made the world's smallest, functional origami fortune-teller, including both symbols and numbers.

Organ Playing

Longest
60 hours. On September 1, 1994, Jürgen Sinner of Germany, began his marathon street organ-playing attempt. BOAR

Pancake Tossing

Highest

Cynthia L. Morrison
The World's Preeminent
Female Escapologist

48-year-old female.
West Palm Beach, FL, USA.
Single.
Stunt performer, escape artist,
automotive service specializing in Rolls Royce.
Web: www.geocities.com/Cindini_2000

18 World Records in Escapology, Strength Feats and Stunts.
Among them:

Most weight and distance pulling a vehicle
with hair only: 6,126 lb. for 112 feet

Fastest handcuff escape on land: 2.5 seconds;
underwater: 3.16 seconds

Fastest female straitjacket escape: 14.66 seconds;
inverted: 19.10 seconds.

Most weight held while laying on broken
glass: 938 lb.

Most weight held while laying between broken glass and a bed of nails: 502 lb.

Cynthia Morrison was aware of her appetite for challenging the unusual and "larger than life" when, as a child, she set her sights on becoming a matador. Lack of instruction and livestock and then a developing compassion for the bulls' inhumane demise kept Cynthia from pursuing the event. This personality characteristic has stayed with her throughout life and led her to pursue such events as power lifting, and becoming the first woman to compete in the Highland Games' heavy athletic events in Scotland (1994). Cynthia began jousting and won the 1999 and 2000 International Jousting Championships in Colorado.

In 1997, she stumbled upon the performing art of escapology and now is believed to be the only female escape artist to achieve jail escapes, thus living up to her stage name, "The Great Cindini." Cynthia's escapes have been featured by Ripley's Believe It or Not! and a world record show on Canada's Discovery Channel. Notably, she's performed in the Congress of Strange and Unusual during RHR's World Record Show at Sideshows by the Seashore at Coney Island, NY, USA. Cynthia's sideshow act includes knife throwing, fire eating, and the bullet-catch with her mouth.

28.21 feet. The highest a pancake has been tossed and re-caught in a pan is 28.21 feet (8.60 m) over a bar, by Jean-Marie Livonnen of France. BOAR

Paper Folding

Ships
200,000. He arranges them in colorful images and sells them. John Brown. ASIA BOOK OF RECORDS

Paperclip Chain

Most
111,000. The longest paperclip chain constructed by a single person was made by Thomas Paul of Germany, in 1992. His 8,202 foot (2,500 m) chain was made from 111,000 paperclips. For his attempt, he used vacation time from school. BOAR

Patents

Most
7,285. 1,688 are registered in the USA. Shunpei Yamazaki.

Pea Pushing

Nose
100 yards: Fastest: 4 minutes, 30 seconds. Helen McDonald performed this task in 4 minutes, 30 seconds. BOAR

1 mile: Fastest: 6 hours, 40 minutes. Helen McDonald performed this task in 6 hours, 40 minutes. BOAR

Longest: 2 miles 50 yards. Alex Crawford performed this task in 16 hours. BOAR

Two Miles

Fastest: 15 hours, 28 minutes. Helga Jansens performed this task in 15 hours, 28 minutes. BOAR

Peanut Rolling

Nose
Distance: 77 miles (124 km). Divya Joshi. ASIA BOOK OF RECORDS

Pipe Smoking

Duration
3 hours, 18 minutes, 15 seconds. The longest period of time a pipe has been smoked by one person without re-lighting is 3 hours, 18 minutes, 15 seconds. Gianfranco Ruscalla of Italy, in 2003. BOAR

Plowing

Duration
300 hours. Demonstrating an amazing feat of endurance, Edgar Heyl from Eggenstein, Germany, plowed for 300 hours, taking a 50 minute rest break after each 10 completed hours. Achieved between November 10 and 22, 1990. BOAR

Poetry Writing

Longest
24,111 words and 104,078 characters. Kobus van Wyk. The poem is entitled, "The Khanya Story," and is written in the quatrain *abab* rhyme scheme.

Most
1 month: 103. Between March 4 and April 3, 2007, Sergey Trofimov of Brooklyn, NY, USA, wrote 103 poems (in the Russian language, no poem less than 4

Mark M. Mosier

45-year-old male.
Sykesville, MD, USA.
Married 19 years.
Professional stuntman, retired correctional officer,
4x4 enthusiast / technician.
Web: www.myspace.com/markmosier
E-mail: mmmtj@comcast.net

World Record:
Longest full-body burn without oxygen:
7 minutes, 44 seconds

Mark Mosier was professionally trained as a stuntman in the early '80s and enjoyed every aspect of stunts. Several years later, when he met professional stuntmen Jeff Wilhelm and Mick Kipp, Mark experienced the thrill of a full-body burn. They decided to make burns their specialty, and over the years, Mark performed many partial and full burns in live performances and movies. He performed one of the first known exposed (fire on skin) burns in a movie.

When Jeff and Mark decided to use their knowledge to set the world record for longest full-body burn without oxygen, they knew there would be many months of research and development as they tried different materials, burn agents, etc., with the purpose of having Mark *on fire from head to toe* for a minimum of 4 minutes—without the use of any breathing apparatus. With Mick and other friends on safety, family members and friends gathered to witness this extraordinary event on November 12, 2006. Under Jeff's coordination, with temperatures reaching 2,300°F, Mark performed a full burn without oxygen for 7 minutes, 44 seconds! He is the world record holder for longest full-body burn without oxygen.

sentences). During the 1 month period, there was not one day in which at least one poem was not written.

6 months: 333. Between September 4, 2006 and March 3, 2007, Sergey Trofimov of Brooklyn, NY, USA, wrote 333 poems (in the Russian language, no poem less than 4 sentences). During this six month period, there was not one day in which at least one poem was not written.

1 year: 742 poems. Between September 4, 2006 and September 3, 2007, Sergey Trofimov of Brooklyn, NY, USA, wrote 742 poems (in the Russian language, no poem less than 4 sentences). During this one year period, there was not one day in which at least one poem was not written.

1,000 poems: Fastest: 1 year, 4 months, 17 days. Between September 4, 2006 and January 20, 2008, Sergey Trofimov of Brooklyn, NY, USA, wrote 1,000 poems (in the Russian language, no poem less than 4 sentences).

Pole Sitting

Longest
196 days. Following the strict rules of the Pole Sitting World Championship, Daniel Baraniuk of Poland, broke the world record in 2002 when he sat on a 2.5 meter pole for 196 days in an amusement park in Soltau, Germany. BOAR

Pom-Pom

Circumference
Largest: 96 inches (record shared with Joan Gould). Natalie D. Gould.

Punk Rock Group

Original members: 4: 31 years. The Adicts: Keith "Monkey" Warren, vocals; Mel Ellis, bass; Pete Dee, guitar; and Kid Dee, drums.

Radio Broadcast

Longest
120 hours. Suresh Joachim.

Radio Interviews
while Suspended in a Cage

98: 21 days: suspended 59 feet. Alastair Galpin. Alastair remained in a suspended cage for 21 days and conducted 98 radio interviews from countries around the world.

Rats Down Tights

Most
47. Ken Edwards.

Rhinestones

Most
31,680 on the body of Alastair Galpin by Mem Bourke, between November 12 and 14, 2006 at the Design to Wear in Auckland, New Zealand.

Rice

Most Letters Written on a Single Grain of Rice
813. Dipak Syal. ASIA BOOK OF RECORDS

Rocking Chair

Marathon
Longest: 75 hours. Suresh Joachim.

Paul Nardizzi
The World's Fastest Stand-up Comic

40-year-old male.
Framingham, MA, USA.
Married with four children.
Stand-up comedian.
Web: www.paulnardizzi.com
E-mail: info@paulnardizzi.com

World Record:
Most stand-up punch lines in an 8-minute set:
73

Paul Nardizzi started performing comedy in 1990, quickly establishing himself as having extremely rapid-fire delivery and a high rate of punch lines. He continued to write new material but also constantly updated the older jokes, infusing them with more punch lines, for example, a joke originally with two punch lines would have upwards of four to six punch lines.

Paul's "Light Block Milk" bit, which quickly gained a listing on XM's top 100 listener request list, has ten punch lines after the setup.

His act has allowed him to appear on *Late Night with Conan O'Brien* three times, as well as Comedy Central's *Shorties Watching Shorties*, *The Best Damn Sports Show Period*, and in 2001, he won the Boston International Comedy Festival. Paul set the punch line record at a comedy club in Pittsfield, MA, USA, in 2006. The record setting performance was an eight minute stand-up set that had 73 original jokes written by himself, each producing a distinct and separate burst of loud laughter from the audience. That is an average of just over nine jokes every minute or one every 6.6 seconds.

Roller Coaster Riding

Distance

18,642 miles. Richard Rodriguez. One year later, Richard set an even more challenging record. From July 10 to August 28, 2003, he rode Expedition Ge-Force again, this time almost non-stop—with only a 5 minute per hour break time allowed. In 49 days, he rode 18,642 miles (30,000 km). BOAR

Duration

1,112 hours. Starting May 23, 2002, multiple record breaker for marathon roller coaster riding, Richard Rodriguez, 44, a teacher from Chicago, Illinois, USA, spent 104 days on the roller coaster, Expedition Ge-Force, in Haßloch, Germany. According to the rules, he had to ride the coaster non-stop for 10 hours, each and every day. However, during the summer nights at Holiday Park, Richard spent 15 hours a day on the ride. The total riding time was 1,112 hours, which equates to 20 circuits every hour and a total number of 22,240 circuits on Expedition GeForce. BOAR

Roller Skating

1,000 Kilometers

84 hours, 56 minutes, 14 seconds. It took Mathias Lillge of Germany, exactly 84:56:14 to skate 1,000 kilometers on in-line skates at Bad Freienwalde from June 2 to 5, 2005. BOAR

Rubber Bands

Furthest Shooting

99 feet. Leo Clouser.

Worn on Head

Most: 66. Time: 1 minute. Alastair Galpin.

Santa Letter

Most Names and Wishes
495. Scot Grassette. One piece of paper, 23 feet 8 inches wide by 131 inches long, weighing 42 lb. and using 288 stamps, was signed by 495 people. The names and wishes were to scale 10 inches high with 2 inch spaces between lines. The event was organized by and took place at Rumford Maine Mountain Valley High School.

Sermon

Longest
93 hours. Donald "Spiderman" Thomas.

Shopping Trolley Run

Team
24 hours: 141,328 meters. The world record was broken by Frans Pretorius and Shaun Jan Johan Meintjies of South Africa. From September 3 to 4, 2004, they covered a total distance of 141,328 meters in 24 hours at City Mall Klerksdorp. BOAR

Sideshow Bally

Consecutive, non-stop 3 minute ballys: 6 hours, 43 minutes: 150. Scott Baker. Each bally included the Human Blockhead with an 8-inch screwdriver.

Sign Language

Duration
12 hours. Vicar Michael Sabell set a world record for non-stop "talking" in sign language, on November 2, 1987 in Sheffield, Yorkshire, United Kingdom, of

Rodolfo Reyes

43-year-old male.
Kitzingen, Germany.
Married.
Professional handstand and head-balance artist.
Web: www.rodolforeyes.com.
E-mail: info@rodolforeyes.com, rodolforeyes@gmx.de

World Record:
World's fastest vertical body one-handed hop

Rodolfo Reyes started training at the age of 6, first learning how to hold a good handstand. It took him 2 years to have perfect vertical position. After that came the juggling side, and finally, the idea to jump on one hand. Rodolfo has been performing as a professional acrobat since the age of 17 and has appeared all over Europe and Asia. He is the winner of many awards: Artist of the Year (2001) in Germany, a TV award in Genova, Italy, Artistic Award for

Best Circus Act in Paris, and Juggler of the Year (2007) in Germany.

Rodolfo's act is unique around the world; it was first performed by his father, who was his teacher for eleven years. Rodolfo's parents traveled with him all over the world until he finally met his wife. He has appeared in numerous TV shows in Italy, Spain, Portugal, France, and England on *Paul Daniels Magic Show*, a show on which he was honored to make a repeat performance of his act a few years later. Trade fairs, theme parks, and car presentations are also in his repertoire. Rodolfo thinks one of his biggest challenges is a record that he now holds: 10 meters jumping on one hand. It involves a lot of conditioning.

12 hours exactly. In doing so, he raised £400 for the deaf. BOAR

Non-Stop
132 hours, 45 minutes. Eamonn McGirr from County Derry, Ireland, holds the record for non-stop signing, a record he's held on and off since the 1970s, when he started the record with a time of 132 hours, 45 minutes (5½ days). Beginning on January 10, 1996, Eamonn broke the record live on television on January 21, 1996 during a telethon to benefit the Centre for the Disabled, the record being exactly 11 days, beating the previous record of 10 days, 22 hours. BOAR

Snails

Face
10 seconds: 8. Alastair Galpin.

Snakes

In Mouth
Most: 8 live snakes by the tails. Time: 12.5 seconds. Deepak Kumar. ASIA BOOK OF RECORDS

Kissing
10 Monocle Cobras and a King Cobra consecutively. Deepak Kumar. ASIA BOOK OF RECORDS

Socks

Worn on 1 Foot
74. Alastair Galpin. At the Design to Wear on November 7, 2006 in Auckland, New Zealand.

Song Writing

Fastest Song to Nationally Syndicated Radio Broadcast

24 hours. Mark Shepard and Fran Capo. Mark Shepard, ASCAP, co-conceived, wrote, and recorded the song. Fran Capo, ASCAP, publisher, had it broadcast on nationally syndicated radio as "Adventure Girl: The Fran Capo Theme Song."

Spoken Word

Shakespearian Works
110 hours, 46 minutes. Adrian Hilton.

Stamp Loosening

Most
60,171. French stamp collector, Henri Pereira, loosened 60,171 stamps from envelopes in the record time of 47 hours, 48 minutes, September 2–3, 1989. It took the philatelist 15 months to collect all the letters to set the record. BOAR

Staples

To Head
87. Luke "Kyle Buckett" LeBlanc.

Straws in Mouth

Most
260. Marco Hort. BOAR

Sugar Cube Tower

Tallest
57.28 inches (145.5 cm). Mat Hand.

Surgical Gloves

Inflated

Todd Robbins

49-year-old male.
New York, NY, USA.
Married with one child.
Professional sideshow entertainer, author,
theatrical producer, and consultant.
Web: www.toddrobbins.com
E-mail: coneyislandtodd@aol.com

2 World Records:

Fastest time to eat a lightbulb: 50.3 seconds

Lightbulbs eaten over a lifetime: Over 4,000

Todd Robbins has been a professional performer for 30 years. He has appeared on more than 100 TV shows both in the USA and internationally. For 15 years, Todd was associated with Coney Island, NY, USA, first as a sideshow performer, and then he worked his way up to executive director and chairman of the board. He is also one of the producers of

NYC's longest running magic show, "Monday Night Magic."

Todd has performed at events, trade shows, and presentations for major corporations such as: Fujifilm, Amtrak, Salomon Smith Barney, Viva Optical, GE, and others. He has also been associated with Ripley's Believe It or Not for many years, including being the emcee of the Ripley's live show that was presented in Branson, MO, and at various venues across the USA. Todd has also worked with New York's Big Apple Circus and was the online spokesperson for Altoids. As a consultant, Todd has worked with Penn & Teller, Criss Angel, David Blaine, and numerous theatrical, TV, and movie productions. He is the author of the book, *The Modern Con Man: How To Get Something For Nothing*. Todd also created and starred in the Off-Broadway show, *Carnival Knowledge*. His next theater show will be a seance piece called, *The Hauntist*.

2 minutes: 4. Fred Burton inflated 4 surgical gloves to near bursting point in just 2 minutes.

Sword Swallowing

Most Swords in 1 Minute while Inverted
3. On February 1, 2007 Michael Harrison aka "Captain Olav," swallowed 3 swords in one minute while inverted, hanging from his ankles.

3 Minutes
18 swords (sixteen 24-inch plus two 18-inch, of which, the 18-inch swords included two 180° turns). Michael Harrison. Performed September 7, 2006.

Longest
33 inches. George McArthur aka "George the Giant," at 7 feet 4 inches tall, swallowed a 33-inch sword at the Starlight Theatre in Bakersfield, CA, USA, during the filming of the TV show, *More than Human*. Record supplied by Sword Swallowers Association International.

Most
25. Red Stuart swallowed 25 SSAI regulation sized swords, measuring at least 18 inches long by 1.2 inches in width, on September 3, 2005 at the 2005 SSAI Convention in Wilkes-Barre, PA, USA.

Most Simultaneous Sword Swallows
50: 19 people. Dan Meyer, organizer, Dai Andrews, Natasha Veruschka, Red Stuart, Johnny Fox, Zamora (Tim Cridland), Todd Robbins, George (The Giant) McArthur, Lizardman (Erik Sprague), Keith Nelson, Thomas Blackthorne, Petur Pokus Finnbjörnsson, Julia Jewels Strouzer, Bill Berry, Frack (Chad Clos),

Ses Carny (Jesse House), Malakai (Michael Todd), Damien Blade (Danny Snyder), and Roderick Russell.

Most Swords Swallowed in 1 Year
37,500: Brett Loudermilk.

Underwater
Tank of sharks and stingrays. Dan Meyer swallowed a 30-inch sword with 24-inch blade while submerged 20 feet underwater in a tank with 80 sharks and stingrays at Ripley's Aquarium, Myrtle Beach, SC, USA, on May 18, 2007.

Tattoos

Most
Full body. Lucky Diamond Rich.

Most Applied: 1 Hour
110. Tony Clifton. Tony applied 110 tattoos to 105 people in 1 hour.

Texas Skip

Most
11,123. Trick roper Andy Rotz of Hagerstown, MD, USA, broke the record for the most Texas Skips at the Wild West Arts Club Convention 2003 in Las Vegas, NV, USA. The record took over 3 hours, non-stop. BOAR

Text Messaging

Fastest 160-character Message
41.52 seconds. Date: November 12, 2006. Ang Chuang Yang. ASIA BOOK OF RECORDS

Most in 1 Month
555,214. On February 1, 2006, Mr. Nitin Thakor of

Sergey Trofimov
The World's Most Prolific Poet

56-year-old male.
Brooklyn, NY, USA.
Married with one daughter.
Web: www.SergeyTrofimov.com
E-mail: rhymepress@yahoo.com

4 World Records:

Most poems written in 1 month: 103 poems

Most poems written in 6 months: 333 poems

Most poems written in 1 year: 742 poems

Wrote 1,000 poems:
1 year, 4 months, 17 days

Sergey Trofimov never used to write down his poems, they were just in his dreams as he was sleeping and when he awoke, he often didn't remember anything. Then one day, specifically September 1, 2006, after withholding some kind of stress for 1.5 years—built-up emotion—something happening to him. What happened exactly? One day Sergey will write the story about it, but for now, the theme—watch for the woman—shall suffice. On September 4, 2006, Sergey began writing his thoughts as poetry everyday. His first one—at Flagler Beach, Florida—and this poem is the first in his book.

As of February 14, 2009, Sergey has written 1,205 poems. He is publishing the book, *Feelings of Love*, including 444 poems and a CD with 47 poems. His first book is expected for release January 2010. Every book will have CD inside and large amount of CDs will be released for free (about 10,000). Sergey's second book, *MetaHistory*, with a second part, *Fragments of Emotions and/or Pregnancy from Politics*, will also include 444 poems and 2 CDs. All poems are written in Russian.

Gandhinagar, India, established the world record for most text messages in one month with an astonishing 555,214. This averages out to one every 5 seconds over 31 days.

Tie Knotting

Fastest Windsor
4.07 seconds. The fastest time ever recorded for knotting a tie is 4.07 seconds. Hans Georg Prinz of Germany, achieved the record with the "classic" Windsor knot in a contest held in Ingolstadt, Germany, during 2003. BOAR

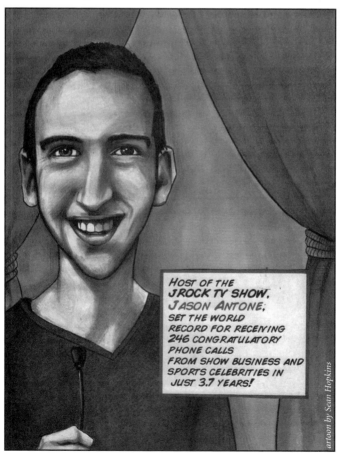

HOST OF THE JROCK TV SHOW, JASON ANTONE, SET THE WORLD RECORD FOR RECEIVING 246 CONGRATULATORY PHONE CALLS FROM SHOW BUSINESS AND SPORTS CELEBRITIES IN JUST 3.7 YEARS!

cartoon by Sean Hopkins

Tightrope Walking

Longest and Highest Blindfolded Sky-walk
800 feet—300 feet above the ground. Jay Cochrane achieved a world record for sky-walking in 1998 when he walked, blindfolded, 300 feet above the lights of Las Vegas between the towers of the Flamingo Hilton, a distance of 800 feet. BOAR

Longest Building-to-Building Sky-walk
2,190 feet. In 2001, Jay sky-walked between two 40-story buildings on opposite sides of the Love River in Kaohsiung, Taiwan, a distance of 2,190 feet in 1 hour, 9 minutes. BOAR

Longest Time on Rope
22 days. Adili Wushouer. ASIA BOOK OF RECORDS

Trampoline

Furthest Trampoline-to-Trampoline Bouncing
15.10 feet. Ukrainian somersault champion Andrey Bezruchenko, a 36-year-old father of one, broke his own world record for bouncing and spinning between two trampolines when he covered a distance of 15.10 feet (4.62 m), smashing his previous best of 14.80 feet (4.52 m). Andrey, a performer with the Moscow State Circus, broke the record during a circus visit to the grounds of Cardiff Castle in Wales, United Kingdom on April 14, 2003. BOAR

Tridem

Smallest Ridden
17.52 inches in length. Ruedi Wenger, together with his daughter, Claudine, and his son, Pascal, performing as the group, Triwengos of Switzerland, rode the

Jayen Varma

47-year-old male.
Cochin, India.
Married.
Professional musician—bass guitar and mridangam.
Web: www.myspace.com/jayenvarma
E-mail: jayenvarma@yahoo.com
jayenvarma@hotmail.com

World Record as World's Fastest Percussive Bassist:
36 percussive notes per second on bass guitar

Jayen Varma has been playing bass guitar for more than two decades and has played on more than 1,000 stages in India. He is the only bass player in the world who plays bass guitar like the Indian percussion instrument tabla or mridangam, with highest pace. Jayen's three finger conventional plucking style ranges from 36 to 48 (at times) notes per second. He is now substituting percussive instruments in Indian classical music with bass guitar. It is becoming a new trend and will be followed by the next generation.

Jayen has been featured in many music magazines and newspapers around the world. Many people tell him that it's unbelievable! He tells them he is ready to perform before them anywhere, provided the number of musical notes he plays chould be checked by a computer. His band is Indian Epics, which is a raga-funk-rock band. Jayen also does a two-piece performance with a raga-rock lead guitar with himself on bass and mridangam. He is set to break his present world record in 2009.

smallest tri-person bicycle on March 29, 1998 at the Tinguley Museum in Basel. With a 17.52 inch long tridem, they rode a distance of 16 meters. BOAR

T-Shirts

Torn
1 minute: 9. Alastair Galpin.

Worn
120. Alastair Galpin. Venue: Collections Clothing Boutique, Henderson, Auckland, New Zealand in May 2006.

Television Watching

Longest
69 hours, 48 minutes. Suresh Joachim.

Typing

1 Finger
Fastest words per minute: 60. The fastest one-finger typist is Farhat Khan of India, who can type 60 words per minute in either Hindi or English, using an electronic typewriter. BOAR

Backward
Fastest: 1 minute: 626. Jens Seiler of Germany, typed backward with a speed of 626 keystrokes per minute on October 4, 1987. He started to train for this record when he had to take part in a beginner's typing course to gain a certification. By this time, Jens was already a skilled typist, it's just that he never had the qualification! BOAR

Duration
276 hours. The marathon record for typing is held

by Gisela Ewald of Germany, with a time of 276 hours. BOAR

Fastest Words per Minute
212. Barbara Blackburn of Salem, Oregon, USA, is the fastest typist in the world. Using the Dvorak Simplified Keyboard, she is able to maintain a speed of 150 wpm for 50 minutes—an amazing 37,500 keystrokes. Her fastest speed was recorded at 212 wpm. The key to her success is the keyboard design. Barbara will type on nothing but the Dvorak keyboard, in preference over the standard QWERTY Keyboard, which has vowels on one side and consonants on the other, with the most frequently used letters in the center row. BOAR

Painting
Largest: 21.4 x 13.3 feet. Uday Mahadeo Talwalkar of India, has typed the largest typewritten "painting"— a portrait of Lata Mangeshkar measuring 21.4 x 13.3 feet. BOAR

Underpants

Worn
20. Alastair Galpin.

Vanilla Bean

Largest Pyramid
264 lb. (120 kg). The vanilla bean pyramid has a 4-sided base of 6 feet (2 m), each side stands 7 feet (2.3 m) tall, it has 7 levels, and contains approximately 33,000 vanilla beans that would stretch over 3.6 miles (5.8 km) if laid out in a straight-line. The

vanilla bean pyramid was established on May 25, 2008 in the city of Papantla, Veracruz, Mexico. The five artisans, Esperanza Castaño Lopez, Adriana Aparicio Gaya, Sergio Nicolas Corona Juarez, Juan Carlos Castaño Lopez, and Ildelfonso Cabañas Ruiz, worked a total of 9 days to complete the project by tying and weaving the vanilla beans one at a time.

Vinyl Record Smashing

Most
20. Time: 30 seconds. Alastair Galpin.

Wedding Bouquet

Caught
38. Jamie Jackson. Jamie caught her first wedding bouquet in 1996.

Wedding Cards

Most Given Out

THE WORLD'S FASTEST MULTI-MILLION DOLLAR DEAL MAKER, *RICARDO BELLINO*, SET THE WORLD RECORD FOR CLOSING A HALF-BILLION DOLLAR DEAL WITH *DONALD TRUMP* IN JUST *3 MINUTES!*

cartoon by Sean Hopkins

1,588. Ken Weatherald of White Rose Wedding Cars, Middlesbrough, UK.

Wedding Party

Largest
128 (includes bride, groom, and all attendants). Suresh Joachim.

Wedding Veil

Longest
1.75 miles. When Eva Hofbauer of Austria, married in June 2004 in Korneuburg, more than 800 children were left outside the church. They were all needed to support Eva's bridal veil—an incredible 1.75 miles of it. BOAR

Whistling

Highest / Lowest Notes
E above middle C and G below middle C. Jennifer Davies of Canada, set the record for whistling both the highest note (the third E above middle C) and the lowest note (the G below middle C) at the Impossibility Challenger Games in Dachau, Germany, on November 6, 2006. BOAR

Yoga

Longest
30 minutes, 22 seconds. Roger Lussi of Switzerland, performed the yoga position Nidrasana for a record time of 30 minutes, 22 seconds. BOAR

Nidrasana Position
5 minutes: 352 passes. Roger Lussi.

CHAPTER 3

Gastronomic

We all eat. Some eat to live and others live to eat. But what about the person who has eaten over 4,000 functioning lightbulbs for entertainment purposes? OK, we'll leave him alone for the moment. What we're really talking about are the people who eat huge quantities of food in lightning speed. Sword swallowers have an expression, "Down the hatch without a scratch." So tell me, where do 66 Nathan's Famous Hot Dogs go in 12 minutes? It seems they should either stretch the stomach to breaking proportions or just pass right on through.

We all drink. Once again, some liquids for survival purposes and others for enjoyment. So how do we explain the guy who downs a pint of ale in 0.45 seconds? He looks normal but when he opens his mouth, it's like looking down the throat of a whale. Liquids just seem to disappear. Oh yea, he does it upside down as well.

NOTE: Because of the prolific eating and drinking records of Peter Dowdeswell, they are reported separately from the remaining gastronomic records.

Drinking

Beer

1 pint: 0.45 second. Peter Dowdeswell.

1 liter: 1.30 seconds. Peter Dowdeswell.

2 pints: 2.30 seconds. Peter Dowdeswell.

3 pints: 4.2 seconds. Peter Dowdeswell.

2 liters: 6 seconds. Peter Dowdeswell.

4 pints: 6.52 seconds. Peter Dowdeswell.

5 pints: 8.90 seconds. Peter Dowdeswell.

6 pints: 12.55 seconds. Peter Dowdeswell.

7 pints: 16.40 seconds. Peter Dowdeswell.

34 pints: 1 hour. Peter Dowdeswell.

90 pints: 3 hours. Peter Dowdeswell.

Through a 6 mm straw: 1 pint: 11.60 seconds. Peter Dowdeswell.

Upside down: 1 pint: 6 seconds. Peter Dowdeswell.

Upside down: 2 pints: 5.2 seconds. Peter Dowdeswell.

Upside down: 3 pints: 7.20 seconds. Peter Dowdeswell.

Upside down: 2 liters: 14.6 seconds. Peter Dowdeswell.

Upside down: 4 pints: 22.1 seconds. Peter Dowdeswell.

Upside down: 5 pints: 29 seconds. Peter Dowdeswell.

Upside down: 6 pints: 32.5 seconds. Peter Dowdeswell.

Upside down: 7 pints: 40.4 seconds. Peter Dowdeswell.

Upside down: 8 pints: 55.6 seconds. Peter Dowdeswell.

Champagne
Upside down: 1 pint: 2.3 seconds. Peter Dowdeswell.

Yard of champagne: 3.5 pints: 14.2 seconds. Peter Dowdeswell.

Milk
1 pint: 2 seconds. Peter Dowdeswell.

2 pints: 3.2 seconds. Peter Dowdeswell.

3 pints: 6 seconds. Peter Dowdeswell.

4 pints: 7.35 seconds. Peter Dowdeswell.

5 pints: 11.45 seconds. Peter Dowdeswell.

6 pints: 16.40 seconds. Peter Dowdeswell.

Upside down: 1 pint: 1.5 seconds. Peter Dowdeswell.

Upside down: 2 pints: 4.6 seconds. Peter Dowdeswell.

Upside down: 3 pints: 8.9 seconds. Peter Dowdeswell.

Upside down: 4 pints: 18.9 seconds. Peter Dowdeswell.

Upside down: 5 pints: 24.4 seconds. Peter Dowdeswell.

Upside down: 6 pints: 30.5 seconds. Peter Dowdeswell.

Upside down: 7 pints: 37.45 seconds. Peter Dowdeswell.

Upside down: 8 pints: 42.40 seconds. Peter Dowdeswell.

Yard of Ale
2.5 pints: 4.9 seconds. Peter Dowdeswell.

3 pints: 5 seconds. Peter Dowdeswell.

4 pints: 8.9 seconds. Peter Dowdeswell.

4.5 pints: 11 seconds. Peter Dowdeswell.

5 pints: 5 seconds. Peter Dowdeswell.

5.5 pints: 12.95 seconds. Peter Dowdeswell.

6 pints: 15.20 seconds. Peter Dowdeswell.

7 pints: 18.26 seconds. Peter Dowdeswell.

7.5 pints: 14 seconds. Peter Dowdeswell.

8 pints: 22.22 seconds. Peter Dowdeswell.

Yard of Coke
4.5 pints: 10 seconds. Peter Dowdeswell.

Eating

Apple Pie
1.5 lb.: 1 minute, 5 seconds. Peter Dowdeswell.

Bananas (peeled)
17: 1 minute, 47 seconds. Peter Dowdeswell.

Brussels Sprouts
1 minute: 32. Peter Dowdeswell.

Carrots (sliced)
2 lb.: 1 minute, 8 seconds. Peter Dowdeswell.

Cheddar Cheese
1 lb.: 1 minute, 13 seconds Peter Dowdeswell.

Chocolate
2 lb.: 4 minutes, 5 seconds. Peter Dowdeswell.

Candy bars: 2 lb.: 4 minutes, 10 seconds. Peter Dowdeswell.

Ferrero Rocher chocolates: 1 minute: 7. Peter Dowdeswell.

Chupa Chups Ice Lolly
48.5 seconds. Reece Nesbitt.

Cockles
2 pints: 1 minute, 8 seconds. Tony Dowdeswell.

Cocktail Sausages
1 minute: 37. Peter Dowdeswell.

Cream Crackers
3 crackers: 18.2 seconds. Peter Dowdeswell.

Custard
2 lb.: 5.4 seconds. Peter Dowdeswell.

Custard Pies
4: 28 seconds. Peter Dowdeswell.

Doughnuts
8 minutes: 113. Peter Dowdeswell.

2-holed doughnuts: 45. 17 minutes, 32 seconds. Peter Dowdeswell.

Eggs
Raw: 13 in 1.04 seconds. Peter Dowdeswell.

Scrambled: 30: 45 seconds. Peter Dowdeswell.

Soft-boiled: 32: 55 seconds. Peter Dowdeswell.

Elvers
1 lb.: 13.7 seconds. Peter Dowdeswell.

Fish and Chips
4 lb. of fish and 4 lb. of chips in 5 minutes, 42 seconds. Peter Dowdeswell.

Fish Fingers
1 lb.: 30 seconds. Peter Dowdeswell.

Gherkins
1 lb.: Fastest: 27.2 seconds. Peter Dowdeswell.

1.2 lb.: 1 minute. Peter Dowdeswell.

Giant Pizzas
6: 1 minute. Peter Dowdeswell.

Grapes
2 lb.: 31.1 seconds. Peter Dowdeswell.

3 lb. (1.36 kg), still attached to stalks, in 31.1 seconds. Peter Dowdeswell.

Haggis
1 lb. 10 oz. (737.5 g) in 49 seconds. Peter Dowdeswell.

Peter Dowdeswell
The World's Most Prolific Eating
and Drinking Champion

68-year-old male.
Earls Barton, UK.
Three children.
Professional eating and drinking champion
Web: www.peterdowdeswell.com
E-mail: pp.dowdeswell1@ntlworld.com

313 World Records. Among them:

Drinking 1 pint of beer: 0.45 seconds

Drinking 90 pints of beer: 3 hours

Eating 14 hard-boiled eggs: 14.42 seconds

Eating 1 lb. of cheddar cheese:
1 minute, 13 seconds

Eating 6 lb. of porridge: 2 minutes, 34 seconds

Peter Dowdeswell has a great appetite for most things in life, and like many people, he enjoys the odd drink and nice meals out. However, he also just happens to be *the* gastronomic champion, with the most eating and drinking records in history—313 (set or broken) in total and unrivaled as of June 2009, 106 of which are listed with Record Holders Republic.

Peter began record breaking in 1974 when, at a fair he beat the world record with his first attempt at drinking a yard of ale in an incredible 5.4 seconds. Since then, he has traveled the world several times over and has appeared on television in the United Kingdom and internationally over 450 times. He has also raised around $10 million for dozens of charities. As a record breaker, Peter has achieved everything possible. He has performed in America, but would like to have the publicity there as he's had in the UK. He believes the key to success is determination and practice.

The reason he drinks beer quickly is because he doesn't like the taste of alcohol. Peter is a teetotaler and only drinks soft drinks when he is at his local pub in Earls Barton, Northampton. He's up to challenge to anyone in the world who thinks they can beat him as the world's number-one eating and drinking champion.

Hamburgers
46.42 lb. (21,100 g) with buns in 9 minutes, 42 seconds. Peter Dowdeswell.

Hot Dogs
5-inch: 12: 8 seconds. Peter Dowdeswell.

5-inch: 16: 26 seconds. Peter Dowdeswell.

5-inch: 22: 1 minute. Peter Dowdeswell.

6-inch: 12: 1 minute. Peter Dowdeswell.

Ice Cream (partly thawed)
12 lb. (5.44 kg) in 45.5 seconds. Peter Dowdeswell.

Jam Sandwiches
6 x 6 inch: 40: 17 minutes, 59.9 seconds. Peter Dowdeswell.

Jelly
Spoon: 18 oz.: Fastest: 22.34 seconds. Peter Dowdeswell.

Mashed Potatoes
3 lb.: 1 minute, 22 seconds. Peter Dowdeswell.

Meat Pies
5.5 oz. (22,156 g) meat pies: 18 minutes, 13.3 seconds. Peter Dowdeswell.

Mince Pies
10: 1 minute, 15 seconds. Peter Dowdeswell.

Pancakes
66: 6-inch pancakes with syrup in 6 minutes, 58.5 seconds. Peter Dowdeswell.

Pickled Onions
24: 1 minute. Peter Dowdeswell.

Pies Soaked in Worcestershire Sauce
4 lb.: 15 minutes. Peter Dowdeswell.

Porridge
6 lb. in 2 minutes, 24 seconds. Peter Dowdeswell.

Prunes
148: 1 minute. Peter Dowdeswell.

Ravioli
5 lb. (170 pieces) in 5 minutes, 34 seconds. Peter Dowdeswell.

Sausage (Boerewors South African)
1 lb.: 1 minute. Peter Dowdeswell.

Shredded Wheat
3: 33.2 seconds. Done without drinking. Peter Dowdeswell.

Shrimp
3 lb.: Fastest: 4 minutes, 8 seconds. Peter Dowdeswell.

202 with 8 pints of jelly: 3 minutes, 10 seconds. Peter Dowdeswell.

Snails
2 lb. in garlic: 3 minutes, 48 seconds. Peter Dowdeswell.

Spaghetti
100 yards: 21.7 seconds. Peter Dowdeswell.

Spaghetti Bolognese: 1 lb.: 25 seconds. Peter Dowdeswell.

Strawberries
2 lb. (907 g) in 12.95 seconds. Peter Dowdeswell.

Sushi
1.5 lb. in 1 minute, 13.5 seconds. Peter Dowdeswell.

Three-course Meal
1 pint oxtail soup, 1 lb. mashed potatoes, ½ lb. sausage, 1 tin of beans, and 50 prunes: 45 seconds. Peter Dowdeswell.

Tomatoes
1 minute: 28. Peter Dowdeswell

Weetabix
4: 36 seconds. Peter Dowdeswell. Done without drinking.

Eating

Asparagus (tempura—deep fried)
6.25 lb.: 10 minutes. Joey Chestnut. April 22, 2006.
IFOCE

Baked Beans
6 lb.: 1 minute, 48 seconds. Don Lerman. IFOCE

Long course: 8.4 lb.: 2 minutes, 47 seconds. Sonya Thomas. August 7, 2004. IFOCE

With cocktail stick: 30 minutes: 2,780. Karen Stevenson. April 4, 1984. BOAR

With cocktail stick: 24 hours: 12,547. Kerry White. August 20, 1984. BOAR

Beans
With cocktail stick: 1 minute: 54. Dean Gould.

With cocktail stick: 3 minutes: 144. Dean Gould.

Beef Tongue
3 lb. 3 oz.: 12 minutes. Dominic Cardo. IFOCE

Birthday Cake
5 lb.: 11 minutes, 26 seconds. May 10, 2005. Richard LeFevre. IFOCE

Black Pudding
3 lb.: 7 minute, 48.9 seconds. Billy "Bunter" Smith. August 1, 1989. BOAR

Blueberry Pie
Hands free: 9.17 lb.: 8 minutes. Patrick Bertoletti. July 28, 2007. IFOCE

Bologna (pork and chicken)
2.76 lb.: 6 minutes. Don Lerman. IFOCE

Brandy Snaps
2 lb.: 14 minutes, 10 seconds. Pauline Adams. January 12, 1990. BOAR

Buffet Food
5.5 lb.: 12 minutes. Crazy Legs Conti. IFOCE

Burritos (Burritoville)
15: 8 minutes. Eric Booker. IFOCE

Butter
7 quarter-pound sticks, salted butter: 5 minutes. Don Lerman.

Cabbage
6 lb. 9 oz.: 9 minutes. Charles Hardy. IFOCE

Cannoli
26: 6 minutes. Cookie Jarvis. September 16, 2005. Record tied by Timothy Janus, September 15, 2006. IFOCE

Cheesecake
11 lb.: 9 minutes. Sonya Thomas. Sept. 26, 2004. IFOCE

Chicken Nuggets
80: 5 minutes. Sonya Thomas. IFOCE

Chicken-fried Steak (11 oz.)
6: 12 minutes. Cookie Jarvis. IFOCE

Chicken Wings
7.5 lb.: 12 minutes. Joey Chestnut. May 21, 2007. IFOCE

Short form: 2 lb. 2.5 oz.: 5 minutes. Cookie Jarvis. IFOCE

Long form: 182: 30 minutes. Joey Chestnut. IFOCE

Chili Cheese Fries
8 lb. 2 oz.: 10 minutes. Sonya Thomas. February 11, 2006. IFOCE

Chili
1.5 gallons: 10 minutes. Richard LeFevre. IFOCE

Chinese Dumplings
91: 8 minutes. Cookie Jarvis. IFOCE

Chocolate Hearts
1 lb. 15.5 oz.: 7 minutes. Patrick Bertoletti. February 13, 2006. IFOCE

Conch Fritters
45: 6 minutes. Joe Menchetti. IFOCE

Corn Dogs (Fletcher's)
12: 10 minutes. Richard LeFevre. September 28, 2003.
IFOCE

Corned Beef and Cabbage
10.63 lb.: 10 minutes. Patrick Bertoletti. March 16, 2007. IFOCE

Corned Beef Hash
4 lb.: 1 minute, 58 seconds. Eric Booker. IFOCE

Corned Beef Sandwiches
8 ounces: 11: 10 minutes. Patrick Bertoletti. January 11, 2006. IFOCE

Cottage Cheese
3 lb.: 4 minutes. Peter Altman of Edgware. March 4, 1984. BOAR

Cow Brains
57 (17.7 lb.): 15 minutes. Takeru Kobayashi. IFOCE

Crab Cakes
46: 10 minutes. Sonya Thomas. April 29, 2006. IFOCE

Cranberry Sauce (jellied)
13.23 lb.: 8 minutes. Juliet Lee. November 22, 2007.
IFOCE

Crawfish
331: 12 minutes. Chris Hendrix. IFOCE

Cucumbers
2.2 lb.: 4 minutes, 2.2 seconds. Jens Rifsdal. December 24, 1988. BOAR

Currants
38: 1 minute: 38. Nathan Gould. Individually with cocktail stick.

Date Nut Bread and Cream Cheese Sandwiches
29.5: 8 minutes. Patrick Bertoletti. December 20, 2006. IFOCE

Doughnuts
1.5 oz.: 22: 1 minute, 39 seconds. Ray Meduna. March 5, 2004. BOAR

Cream filled: 47: 5 minutes. Patrick Bertoletti. March 17, 2007. IFOCE

Glazed: 49: 8 minutes. Eric Booker. IFOCE

Eggs (hard-boiled)
14: 14.2 seconds. John Kenmuir. April 17, 1987. BOAR

65: 6 minutes, 40 seconds. Sonya Thomas. IFOCE

French Fries (Nathan's Famous Crinkle Cut)
4.46 lb.: 6 minutes. Cookie Jarvis. March 31, 2005. IFOCE

Fruitcake (Wegmans)
4 lb. 14¼ oz.: 10 minutes. Sonya Thomas. December 30, 2003. IFOCE

Garlic Cloves
7: 1 minute. Alastair Galpin.

Gelatin Dessert
16 oz. portions: 7: 3 minutes. Steve Lakind. IFOCE

Grits
21 lb.: 10 minutes. Patrick Bertoletti. September 29, 2007. IFOCE

Grapes
133: 3 minutes: Mat Hand.

Smirnoff Twisted V Wild: 8 lb. 15 oz.: 10 minutes. Cookie Jarvis. November 1, 2005. IFOCE

Green Beans (French Cut)
2.71 lb.: 6 minutes. Crazy Legs Conti. IFOCE

Grilled Cheese Sandwiches
47: 10 minutes. Joey Chestnut. June 10, 2006. IFOCE

Gyoza (chicken and vegetable)
212: 10 minutes. Joey Chestnut. August 19, 2006. IFOCE

Ham (sliced)
2 lb. 10 oz.: 5 minutes. Seaver Miller. December 15, 2006. IFOCE

Ham and Potatoes (Easter Feaster meal)
6 lb.: 12 minutes. Cookie Jarvis. IFOCE

Hamburgers
1/4 lb. "Cloud Burgers:" 11: 10 minutes. Don Lerman.
IFOCE

3/4 lb. "Thick Burgers:" 7: 10 minutes. Sonya Thomas.
IFOCE

Big Daddy cheeseburger: 9 lb.: 27 minutes. Sonya Thomas. January 21, 2006. IFOCE

Nathan Gould

13-year-old male.
Felixstowe, Suffolk, UK.
Single.

World Record:
Most currants eaten individually with cocktail stick in 1 minute: 38

Nathan Gould decided to set his first world record when he was 11 years old, inspired by his father, Dean Gould, holder of over 40 world records. Being surrounded by all his father's world record certificates and trophies as well as seeing him on television and in the newspapers gave Nathan great incentive. Although he has the same skill as his father, with dexterity for beermat flipping, coin snatching, etc., Nathan can see it will be a while before he can present a challenge to these records as his hands need to grow. Instead, he went for the currant eating record with a cocktail stick because it is something his father also does with beans and peas. Nathan got lots of currants to practice with, which was cool as he loves them. He has held this record for over a year now and is proud to be in the record book. "It shows you do not have to climb Mount Everest in the quickest time to set or break a world record, just be persistent and good at what you do," said Nathan. In the future, Nathan hopes to hold as many world records as his father and appear on television as well.

Krystal Square: 39: 2 minutes. Bob Shoudt. September 2007. IFOCE

Krystal Square: 103: 8 minutes. Joey Chestnut. October 28, 2007. IFOCE

Hamantaschen (Purim cookies)
50: 6 minutes. Eric Booker. IFOCE

Horseshoe Sandwiches
6 lb. 5 oz.: 12 minutes. Joey Chestnut. IFOCE

Hot Cross Buns
10 oz.: 5 minutes, 10 seconds. Walter Cornelius. April 9, 1971. BOAR

Hot Dogs (Nathan's Famous)
68: 10 minutes. Joey Chestnut. July 4, 2009. IFOCE

Huevos Rancheros
7.75 lb.: 10 minutes. Richard LeFevre. March 18, 2006. IFOCE

Hutspot (potato-based "hotchpotch" bowls of stew)
13: 10 minutes. Henry Hatau. IFOCE

Ice Cream
1 gal. 9 oz.: 12 minutes. Cookie Jarvis. IFOCE

Short form: 1.75 gallons: 8 minutes. Patrick Bertoletti. May 26, 2006. IFOCE

Jalapeño Pickles
177: 15 minutes. Patrick Bertoletti. August 26, 2006. IFOCE

Jalapeño Poppers
118: 10 minutes. Joey Chestnut. April 8, 2006. IFOCE

Jambalaya (crawfish)
9 lb.: 10 minutes. Sonya Thomas. February 24, 2004.
IFOCE

Jelly (with chop sticks)
14 oz.: 1 minute: Alastair Galpin. October 27, 2007.

Key Lime Pie
10.8 lb.: 8 minutes. Patrick Bertoletti. March 21, 2006.
IFOCE

Kolaches (cherry)
44: 8 minutes. Patrick Bertoletti. September 2, 2006.
IFOCE

Lobster Rolls
41: 10 minutes. Takeru Kobayashi. September 23, 2006.

Maine Lobster (Kennebunk)
11.3 lb. of meat from the shell: 44: 12 minutes. Sonya Thomas. August 13, 2005. IFOCE

Matzo Balls (baseball-sized)
21: 5 minutes, 25 seconds. Eric Booker. IFOCE

Mayonnaise
32-ounce bowls: 4: 8 minutes. Oleg Zhornitskiy. IFOCE

Meat Pies
6 oz.: 16: 10 minutes. Boyd Bulot. IFOCE

Meatballs
10 lb. 3 oz.: 12 minutes. Sonya Thomas. December 3, 2005. IFOCE

Native American Fry Bread
9.75 lb.: 8 minutes. Erik "The Red" Denmark. October 28, 2006. IFOCE

Okra (deep fried)
9.75 lb.: 10 minutes. Sonya Thomas. September 16, 2006. IFOCE

Onions
Maui: 8.5 oz.: 3: 1 minute. Eric Booker. August 8, 2004. IFOCE

3 lb. 8.9 oz.: 2 minutes, 2 seconds. Walter Cornelius.

Oysters
Short form: 34 dozen: 8 minutes. Patrick Bertoletti. April 12, 2008. IFOCE

46 dozen: 10 minutes. Sonya Thomas. March 20, 2005. IFOCE

Pancakes and Bacon
3.5 lb.: 12 minutes. Crazy Legs Conti. IFOCE

Pasta (linguini)
6 2/3 lb.: 10 minutes. Cookie Jarvis. IFOCE

Peanut Butter and Jelly Sandwiches
42: 10 minutes. Patrick Bertoletti. August 8, 2007. IFOCE

Peas
1 lb. bowls: 9.5: 12 minutes. Eric Booker. IFOCE

With cocktail stick: 211: 3 minutes. Mat Hand.

Mushy Peas: 10.6 oz.: 1 minute, 8 seconds. Dale Martin.

Pelemeni (Russian dumplings)
274: 6 minutes. Dale Boone. IFOCE

Pickles
Kosher dill: 2.7 lb.: 6 minutes. Brian Seiken. 2005. IFOCE

Sour: 2.99 lb.: 5 minutes. Cookie Jarvis. IFOCE

Pigs Feet and Knuckles
2.89 lb.: 10 minutes. Arturo Rios, Jr. June 23, 2007. IFOCE

Pizza
2 lb.: 29 seconds. John Kenmuir. August 12, 1988. BOAR

Extra large Bacci pizza slices: 7.5: 15 minutes. Richard LeFevre. July 9, 2005. IFOCE

Pizza Hut Pzones
4.82 lb.: 6 minutes. Joey Chestnut. July 10, 2007. IFOCE

Pomme Frites
2 lb. 9 oz.: 8 minutes. Cookie Jarvis. IFOCE

Pork (smoked)
7 lb. 1 oz.: 10 minutes. Richard LeFevre. August 21, 2005. IFOCE

Pork and Beans
84 oz.: 1 minute, 52 seconds. Dale Boone. IFOCE

Pork Ribs
8.4 lb.: 12 minutes. Joey Chestnut. July 16, 2006. IFOCE

Posole
9 lb. 3 oz.: 12 minutes. Patrick Bertoletti. November 18, 2006. IFOCE

Potato Wedges
3.74 lb.: 8 minutes. Tim Brown. October 18, 2007. IFOCE

Pulled Pork Sandwiches
23: 10 minutes. Sonya Thomas. October 3, 2003. IFOCE

Pumpkin Pies (Entenmann's)
4 3/8: 12 minutes. Eric Booker. November 22, 2004. IFOCE

Quesadillas (4-inch)
31.5: 5 minutes. Sonya Thomas. 2005. IFOCE

Raisins
With cocktail stick: 100: 42.5 seconds. Rasmus Rifsdal.

With cocktail stick: 200: 2 minutes, 3.7 seconds. Rasmus Rifsdal.

Ramen Noodles
10.5 lb.: 8 minutes. Timothy Janus. October 27, 2007. IFOCE

Rice
Rice balls: 20 lb.: 30 minutes. Takeru Kobayashi. IFOCE

Using fingers: 2 lb. 8 oz.: 17 minutes, 11 seconds. Parbatainath Basu.

With chopsticks: 3 minutes: 174 grains. Park Hwa-Jin. November 21, 2004. BOAR

Sausages
Bratwurst (Johnsonville): 58: 10 minutes. Takeru Kobayashi. August 5, 2006. IFOCE

Hot sausages: 2 oz.: 10 minutes, 11.8 seconds. Walter Cornelius.

Raw chain sausages: 5.36 meters of 2 oz. sausages: 5 minutes, 34 seconds. Walter Cornelius.

Raw sausages: 47: 2 oz.: 8 minutes, 30 seconds. Walter Cornelius.

Reindeer sausages (Glacier Brewhouse): 28: 10 minutes. Dale Boone. IFOCE

Sausages (Armour Vienna): 8.31 lb.: 10 minutes. Sonya Thomas. May 28, 2005. IFOCE

Sausage sandwiches: 13.25 lb.: 12 minutes. Chip "Burger" Simpson. August 26, 2006. IFOCE

Shoofly Pie
11.1 lb.: 8 minutes. Patrick Bertoletti. June 23, 2007.
IFOCE

Shrimp
4 lb. 15 oz.: 12 minutes. Erik "The Red" Denmark. September 22, 2006. IFOCE

Spam
6 lb.: 12 minutes. Richard LeFevre. April 3, 2004. IFOCE

Strawberry Rhubarb Pie
7.9 lb.: 8 minutes. Patrick Bertoletti. July 29, 2006. IFOCE

Strawberry Shortcake
15.25 lb.: 8 minutes. Patrick Bertoletti. June 17, 2007.
IFOCE

Sultanas
100: 1 minute, 44.65 seconds. Mark Say. November
16, 1985. BOAR

Sweet Corn
Ears: 34.75: 12 minutes. Crazy Legs Conti. April 29,
2007. IFOCE

Single kernel: 1 minute: 47. David Downes, Jr.

Sweet Potato Casserole
8.62 lb.: 11 minutes. Sonya Thomas. October 20,
2004. IFOCE

Tacos (soft, chicken)
48: 11 minutes. Sonya Thomas. September 29, 2004.
IFOCE

Tamales
71: 12 minutes. Timothy Janus. September 1, 2007.
IFOCE

Tex-Mex Rolls
30: 12 minutes. Richard LeFevre. March 12, 2005.
IFOCE

Tiramisu
4 lb.: 6 minutes. Timothy Janus. March 5, 2005. IFOCE

Toasted Ravioli
4 lb.: 12 minutes. Sonya Thomas. November 20, 2004. IFOCE

Turkey
4 lb. 12.8 oz.: 12 minutes. Patrick Bertoletti. November 22, 2006. IFOCE

Whole, short form: 6.91 lb.: 8 minutes. Patrick Bertoletti. November 22, 2007. IFOCE

Waffles
8 oz.: 29: 10 minutes. Patrick Bertoletti. October 7, 2007. IFOCE

Watermelon
13.22 lb.: 15 minutes. July 30, 2005. Jim Reeves. Brookville Community Picnic. IFOCE

Yorkshire Pudding
3 lb.: 7 minutes, 22 seconds. John Davidson. March, 18 1986. BOAR

CHAPTER 4

Memory

Memory is a fascinating thing. Some people have it and some people don't—often with wide variations in between. Memory is a person's ability to store, retain, and retrieve information either short- or long-term. An individual may have the inherent ability to remember or recall things or lists of objects that happened years ago. And yet another may not remember what it was he or she walked into a room looking for. Fortunately for some, memory is a trainable skill. Mnemonics (memory aids), in the form of short poems or visualizations, are often credited as allowing people to memorize lists, faces, and names.

Memory records vary from the ability to recite and/or calculate the lengthy decimal places of pi to the ability to quickly study the colors of a Rubik's cube, don a blindfold, and solve the cube in a matter of seconds. Other amazing memory feats include the ability to recite back a shuffled deck of cards after a mere "glance" or the ability to solve complex mathematical problems in literally fractions of a second.

Calendar

Year
365 random days of the week. 214 seconds. Matthias Kesselschlager. BOAR

Century
20 random dates. 17.9 seconds. Matthias Kesselschlager. BOAR

5 Centuries (1600–2100)
Random days of the week. 1 minute. 56. Yusnier Viera Romero. (Subsequently tied by Jan van Koningsveld.) BOAR

10 Billion Years
60 random dates: 0000 to 10 billion: 1 minute: 60. Sababbi Mangal.

10 Billion Year Calendar
A mathematical formula has been devised to calculate any day from zero to 10 billion. Kapil Kalra.

Chemical Elements

Unnamed
1,082. Jasper Medellin of LaRue, of Texas, USA, named all undiscovered chemical elements with atomic numbers from 118 through 1,200 on November 1 and 2, 2006.

Creighton Carvello

64-year-old male.
Middlesbrough, UK.
Single with no children.
Memory man, adviser for memory records, RHR.
Web: www.memorablecarvello.co.uk
E-mail: creighton@memorablecarvello.co.uk

World Records:
Most numbers in pi matrix: 11,000
Most FA Cup soccer facts: 4,000

Creighton Carvello discovered his amazing memory when he was about 7 years old. He started collecting soccer cards and tried to memorize them all. His friends were amazed at how he could remember, in order, hundreds of cards. Creighton broke his first world record when he was in his mid 30's in 1980 when he memorized and recalled from memory, the first 20,013 digits of pi with no errors. This was achieved at Saltscar School in Redcar, Middlesbrough, United Kingdom.

In 1987, Creighton memorized the order of six packs of shuffled playing cards after being seen once only. In 1992, he memorized one pack of shuffled cards in 2 minutes, 17 seconds. He also went on to memorize 18 random digits after being flashed up on a screen in 4 seconds, then 13 digits in 1 second. He has been called the original memory man since the early 1980s.

Creighton's television appearances have stretched from all four corners of the world, including France, Germany, Japan, and Thailand, to name a few, as well as many appearances on British television. He has recently suffered a massive stroke and is presently recovering slowly in the hospital but hopes to be back home in the near future, when he plans to start up his memory record breaking. Creighton is very proud of what he has achieved as a world record memory man and knows his family and friends are as well.

Chess

Blindfolded
52 games. In 1952, Janos Flesch of Hungary, played 52 games of chess, blindfolded. Relying on memory of the games, he won 31, drew 18, and lost just 3. BOAR

Consecutive Games Played
1,131. On August 1, 2005, Zsuza Polgar of the USA, played 1,131 games against 551 opponents. The final score was 1,112 wins, 16 draws, and 3 losses. BOAR

Simultaneous Matches
326. On August 1, 2005, Zsuzsa Polgar of the USA, played against 326 players simultaneously in 16 hours, 30 minutes at the Gardens Mall in Palm Beach Gardens, Florida. He won 309, drew 14, and lost just 3 games! BOAR

Concentration Playing

Largest / Longest
2,400 cards. The largest game of Concentration (the card matching game that is also known as Memory) was played on June 17, 1986 by Julie Glowka, Christiane Dein, Erik Scheid, and Georg Lay. In 18 hours, 56 minutes, the four students of mathematics at the University Saarbrücken in Germany, found 1,200 matching pairs among 2,400 cards. BOAR

Draughts

Blindfolded
22 games. Since 1982, Ton Sijbrands of the Netherlands, has held the record for the most games of draughts played from memory whilst blindfolded.

The current record of 22 was achieved on December 21, 2002. Ton won 17, drew 5, and lost none. BOAR

Mathematical Calculations

13th Root of 100 Digit Number
13.55 seconds. Alexis Lemaire.

Adding 100 Random Digits in 1 minute
19.23 seconds. Alberto Coto Garcia.

Memorization

100 Digits
Fastest: 50.1 seconds. Ramón Campayo of Spain, needed only 50.1 seconds to memorize 100 digits on September 9, 2006 in Buenos Aires. BOAR

100 Random Mobile Numbers with Names
19 minutes, 38 seconds. Guriqbal Singh.

100 Random Objects
9 minutes, 49 seconds. Nandini Sankhla.

Binary Digits
1 second: 30. Ramón Campayo.

2 seconds: 42. Ramón Campayo.

3 seconds: 48. Ramón Campayo.

Screen flash: 1 second: 46. Ramón Campayo of Spain, June 8, 2006 in Pelhrimov, Czech Republic. BOAR

Screen flash: 2 seconds: 54. Ramón Campayo of Spain, June 8, 2007 in Pelhrimov, Czech Republic. BOAR

Screen flash: 3 seconds: 62. Ramón Campayo of Spain, November 5, 2006 in Dachau, Germany. BOAR

1 minute: 240. Itay Avigdor of Israel, memorized 240 binary digits within 1 minute on June 22, 2006 in Ramat Gan, Israel. This has been a really remarkable improvement on the old record of 162, set by Gunther Karsten of Germany, on September 4, 2005. BOAR

5 minutes: 795. Ben Pridmore memorized 795 binary digits in 5 minutes at the UK Memory Championship in Shropshire on July 14, 2007. BOAR

30 minutes: 4,140. At the 2007 Memory World Championship in Manama, Bahrain, Ben Pridmore of the United Kingdom, remembered 4,140 random binary digits in 30 minutes. BOAR

Dictionary
All 80,000 entries from the *Oxford Advanced Learners Dictionary*. Mahaveeer Jain. ASIA BOOK OF RECORDS

FA Cup Facts
4,000. Creighton Carvello.

ISD Codes, Capitals, and Currencies of All Countries in the World, Recalling at an Average Speed of 0.08 Seconds per One, with 100% Accuracy
Mohd Faisal. Venue: Sambhal, Moradabad, Uttar Pradesh, India, July 2007.

Names and Faces
156. Andi Bell.

Pi
1,000 places: Fastest time: 8 minutes, 14 seconds. Dean Gould. Great Eastern Square, Felixstowe, United Kingdom on May 14, 1998.

Digits: 67,890. The most digits of pi ever recited without a mistake was achieved on November 20, 2005 by Chao Lu of China, with an amazing 67,890 digits. BOAR

Pi Matrix
Most numbers: 11,000. Creighton Carvello.

Pi Reciting
Time: 2 minutes. Total: 179 with no errors. Dean Gould.

Playing Cards
84.24 seconds, then recalled forward and backward with 100 percent accuracy. Krishan Chahal.

1 minute: a shuffled pack was memorized. Cards recalled successfully at random positions within deck. Nitin Grover.

1 deck: Fastest: 26.28 seconds. Ben Pridmore of the United Kingdom, needed only 26.28 seconds to memorize a shuffled deck of 52 playing cards at the UK Open Memory Championship in Shropshire, July 14, 2007. BOAR

Random Decimal Numbers
1 minute: 102. Dr. Gunther Karsten of Germany, was able to memorize 102 decimal digits within 1 minute. Afterward, he recalled all these digits without a single error on January 31, 2007 at Grand Hyatt Hotel in Hong Kong. BOAR

1 hour: 1,949. The record for the most numbers recalled after memorizing as many digits as possible in 1 hour is 1,949, by Dr. Gunther Karsten of Germany,

Kapil Kalra

23-year-old male.
Dehradun, India.
Single.
Head of Department, Pharmacy, M. Pharma.
Web: www.rhrindianrecords.com
E-mail: kapil752003@yahoo.com

3 World Records:

10 billion year calendar

Trigonometric table in a half page

Unshuffling playing cards in 38 seconds

Kapil Kalra's first record is a written mathematical formula that has been devised to 10 billion years. He was inspired by a young boy who made a 10,000 year calendar. After seeing this calendar, Kapil started his journey of world records and made a 10 billion year calendar. Presently, he holds three records with Record Holders Republic. He reviews Indian record submissions as the Indian representative of Record Holders Republic. As President of Indian Records, he does various national and international media interviews about Indian world records.

Kapil has been awarded the title, "Einstein of India," by National News Channel. After his 10 billion year calendar, Kapil made two other records: Trigonometric table in a half page (basically a sine and cosine theta table) and the other is unshuffling a mixed deck of playing cards in 38 seconds, ordering them from Ace through King, by suit, with one hand only. In the future, he plans on converting a log table in visiting card form. Presently, Kapil is working on converting liquid alcohol to solid alcohol. He has already prepared solid alcohol polymer from liquid alcohol. Moreover, he is the only Indian person to hold records for three feats with Record Holders Republic.

at the 2005 world championship in Oxford, United Kingdom. At the German Memory Championship 2007 in Tuttlingen, he set the record for 30 minutes with 1,160 digits memorized and recalled. BOAR

5 minutes: 396. Andi Bell of the United Kingdom, memorized a total of 396 digits in 5 minutes at the 2007 German Memory Championship in Tuttlingen. BOAR

30 minutes: 1,200. Lorendana Feuchter.

Screen flash: 1 second: 19. Ramón Campayo of Spain, November 6, 2005 in Dachau, Germany. BOAR

Screen flash: 4 seconds: 26. Ramón Campayo of Spain, June 8, 2006 in Pelhrimov, Czech Republic. BOAR

Telephone Numbers
16,000. Tom Morton.

Word Meaning Recollection
1 minute: 10. Taken randomly from the *Oxford Dictionary*. New Delhi, India on February 11, 2008. Roy Neerja. ASIA BOOK OF RECORDS

Words
15 minutes: 255. Boris-Nikolai Konrad of Germany, memorized an amazing 227 randomly selected words in 15 minutes. BOAR

Mental Calculations

Adding Ten 10-digit Numbers
4 minutes 26 seconds. Alberto Coto. Ten mental calculation tasks of the type "add ten 10-digit numbers" without an error. BOAR

Multiplication

10 Tasks with 5 Digit Numbers
3 minutes, 6 seconds. Jan van Koningsveld of Germany, holds the corresponding record for 5-digit numbers with a time of 3 minutes, 6 seconds, achieved on November 25, 2005 in Emden, Germany. BOAR

10 Tasks with 8 Digit Numbers
8 minutes 25 seconds. Alberto Coto. Ten mental calculation tasks of the type "multiply two 8-digit numbers" without an error. BOAR

Fastest Mentally
2 random 8 digit numbers in 50.88 seconds. Jan van Koningsveld.

Reading

Fastest
1 hour: 80,000 words. Maria Teresa. ASIA BOOK OF RECORDS

Rubik's Cube

24 Hours
3,390. Zbigniew Zborowski of Poland, June 23–24, 2006. BOAR

4 x 4 x 4 Cube
43.70 seconds. Erik Akkersdijk. BOAR

5 x 5 x 5 Cube
1 minute, 28.66 seconds. Erik Akkersdijk of the Netherlands, at the Belgian Open on February 3, 2008 in Leuven. BOAR

Blindfolded
10. Dennis Strehlau of Germany, at the Belgian Open on February 2, 2008 in Leuven. BOAR

Fastest (including memorization): 1 minute, 10.27 seconds, Danyang Chen of China, at the Beijing Open on December 15, 2007. BOAR

Including memorization: 1 minute, 0.62 seconds. Alexander Yu of the USA, solved a Rubik's Cube in 1 minute, 0.62 seconds while blindfolded. This includes the time to study the cube as well as the time to solve it. The record was set at the Princeton Open contest on March 22, 2008. BOAR

Fastest (not including memorization): 23.06 seconds. Clément Gallet of France, at the European Rubik's Cube Championship, Paris 2006. BOAR

4 x 4 x 4 cube: Fastest (including memorization): 6 minutes, 20.96 seconds. Chris Hardwick of the USA, at the Virginia Open on November 24, 2007. BOAR

5 x 5 x 5 cube: Fastest (including memorization): 19 minutes, 55 seconds. Chris Hardwick of the USA, at Chattahoochee, March 24, 2007. BOAR

Fastest
9.18 seconds. The best time for restoring the cube in an official championship is 9.18 seconds by Edouard Chambon of France, at the Murcia Open Championship on February 23, 2008 in Puente Tocinos, Spain. BOAR

Feet Only
39.88 seconds. Anssi Vanhala of Finland, at the Finnish Open 2007, Helsinki. BOAR

One-Handed
Fastest: 23.76 seconds. Shotaro Makisumi of Japan,

solved a Rubik's cube, one-handed, in 23.76 seconds at the Horace Mann Spring Tournament on May 28, 2005. BOAR

Two-Handed
Fastest: 15.81 seconds. Thibaut Jacquinot of France. The Murcia Open 2007 in Puente Tocinos, Spain. BOAR

Robot
64 seconds. Peter Redmond (developer). BOAR

Spelling

Reverse
3 minutes: 50 words. Raghav Srivathsav. ASIA BOOK OF RECORDS

Trigonometric Table

On Half a Page
Kapil Kalra.

Ralf Laue

40-year-old male.
Leipzig, Germany.
Married with two children.
Mathematics specialist,
president of Rekord-Klub Saxonia and BOAR.
Web: www.recordholders.org
Email: info@recordholders.org

World Record Holder for Dexterity, Balance, and Memory.
Among them:

Fastest pancake flipper

Largest fan of cards

Longest distance tiddlywinking

Ralf Laue has been interested in world records since the age of 12. Since then, he has collected the largest archive and data of world record information, second only to Guinness. Ralf broke his first record in 1986 with the largest fan of playing cards held in one hand. Since then, he's broken over 20 records to date. When not working on world records, he teaches computer science at the University of Leipzig, Germany, and works as a computer specialist. In 1988, he formed Rekord-Klub Saxonia, an international club whose membership is composed of world record holders. Ralf authored *The Book of Alternative Records* (in both English and German) with Dean and Philip Gould from Record Holders Republic.

One of Ralf's greatest accomplishments for record holders is to organize several record festivals as well as the Mental Calculation World Cup. Record breakers from all over the world meet at these occasions. He likes to practice records that can be tried at home with little preparation. His most difficult record was solving 3 Rubik's cubes from memory while blindfolded. Ralf says he finds it difficult to break his own records as they are not so challenging as beating those of others.

Chapter 5

Sports

Sports are usually viewed as participating in an activity in which some type of exertion or skill is played out by one or more people, individually or as a team. Almost everyone plays or has played sports sometime in their lives. Some like to play soccer, baseball, cycle a bike, billiards, or golf. Others enjoy twirling a Hula-hoop or even three-legged racing. To some, it's just a game. To others, it's viewed entirely different. There's no need to compete with anyone else. Competing with themselves is quite good enough.

For example, why play the game of tennis when you could stand there and bounce a ball on the edge of a racket, over and over and over? Why just look at a soccer ball as a piece of sporting equipment to kick back and forth from one end of the field to the other when you could bounce it off your head, endlessly?

Baseballs

Held in One Hand, Palm Down
4. Alastair Galpin.

Held in One Hand with Baseball Glove
10. Alastair Galpin.

Basketball

Blindfolded
10 baskets: 2 minutes, 42 seconds. The fastest time to achieve 10 baskets whilst totally blindfolded is 2 minutes, 42 seconds by Sadie Edwards of Birmingham, United Kingdom, on the television show, *You Bet*, screened on February 16, 1989 in the United Kingdom. BOAR

Dribbling
24 hours: 108.4 miles. Ultra-marathon runner Tyler Curiel, broke the record for dribbling a basketball whilst running over a 24-hour period. The event called, "Bounce for Life," was held to support research in Curiel's lab at Tulane University School of Medicine, New Orleans, USA, where he is the chief of hematology and medical oncology. BOAR

Heading
Most consecutive baskets scored: 17. Jacek Roszkowski.

Hoops
Fastest in 48 Contiguous US States: 8 days 5 hours 33 minutes. Richard Paff, John Baker, and Jack Davis. Richard Paff, John Baker, and Jack Davis drove their car through each of the 48 contiguous US States so that each of them successfully completed no less than 1 basketball hoop in each state.

Scoring
9 baskets in 1 minute, dribbling 10 meters and scoring all. Jermaine Bernard. This was then equaled by Milo Hodge at a super stars competition in Ipswich on July 20, 2003.

Bathtub

English Channel Crossing
Fastest: 9 hours, 6 minutes. Tim Fitzhigham. Tim rowed a copper bathtub across the English Channel in 9 hours, 6 minutes.

Sailing Longest
1,800 miles. October 9, 1983, Bill Neal of Salcombe, Devon, United Kingdom, completed a 1,800 mile (2,900 km) sail from London to Korkta, Finland, in a fiberglass, Jacuzzi-type bathtub, accompanied by three friends in a support boat. Bill's journey took almost 4 months to complete. BOAR

Billiard Ball

Jump
Highest: 13.8 inches. Dominik Halamka of Prague, Czech Republic, holds the record for billiard ball high jump. He shot a ball such that it cleared a 13.8 inch bar. BOAR

Bowling

10 Pin
Longest marathon: 100 hours. Suresh Joachim.

Brick Throwing

Furthest

148 feet 6 inches. At the Alternative Olympics held in Hull, Humberside, United Kingdom, on September 20, 1988, Dave Wattle of Sheffield threw a 5 lb. (2.268 kg) building brick, 148 feet 6 inches. BOAR

Car Hurdling

Width-ways
101: 38 minutes. Jeff Clay. ASIA BOOK OF RECORDS

Chariot Challenge

42.77 seconds. Sam Dobin. This is the famous Trinity Great Court Run, which is run by first-year students of Trinity College once a year. A handkerchief is dropped before the start. The run, a distance of 401 yards around the court, has been impossible in the past, even by professionals.

Custard-Filled Wellie Relay Marathon

27 people. Time: 3 hours, 3 minutes, 26.6 seconds. Teams: Brentwood Police and Gateway International. BOAR

Cycling

Acrobatic
Distance: 3,125 meters. Martina Štepánková of the Czech Republic, has a world record for cycling not in the usual way, but by standing on her hands (one hand on the saddle, the other one at the handlebar). BOAR

Backward
1 hour: Distance: 31 miles. On May 24, 2003, Markus Riese of Germany, broke the distance record

for riding a bicycle backward in 1 hour when he achieved a distance of 18 miles. He continued cycling until he broke the 31 mile (50 km) record, recording a world record time of 1:46:59. BOAR

1 hour: Fastest: 16.72 miles (26.9 km). Pieter de Hart.

31.08 miles (50 km): Fastest: 2 hours, 8 minutes. Pieter de Hart.

100 km: Fastest: 4 hours, 5 minutes, 1 second. On August 11, 1985, Alan Pierce of Australia, rode a cycle backwards over the distance of 62 miles (100 km). BOAR

Greatest distance: 91.43 miles. During 1992, in Lucani, Serbia, Goran Alempijevic of Serbia, rode a cycle backward 91.43 miles in 6½ hours. BOAR

Fastest
167.05 mph. Fred Rompelberg of the Netherlands, rode a bicycle at a speed of 167.05 mph (268.831 km/h) behind a car used as a pacemaker, recording a time of 13.3 seconds for the distance of 0.62 miles (1 km), and 21.15 seconds for 1 mile (1.60 km). This record was achieved in Bonneville, Salt Lake, USA on October 3, 1995. BOAR

Playing Violin
Backward: 37.56 miles. During 1987, Christian Patzig of Germany, rode a bicycle backward whilst playing the violin for a distance of 37.56 miles in a time of 5 hours, 8 minutes. During the record attempt, Christian experienced no problems. However during a practice session, this was not the case. He ran over a policeman! BOAR

Longest duration: 5 hours, 9 minutes. Christian Adams.

Upstairs
1 hour: 1,600 stairs. Hugues Richard of France, pedaled a mountain bike up 1,600 stairs in Montmartre, Paris within 1 hour on October 5, 2000. BOAR

Darts

1,320: Center bull's-eyes: 10 hours. John Lowe.

Fastest
1,001 in 2 minutes, 32 seconds. Dean Gould. Felixstowe, United Kingdom, on November 29, 1996.

301 in 36 seconds. Dean Gould. Ipswich, United Kingdom on October 31, 1996.

Using 6-inch Nails
7 hours: 4,746. We have all heard stories about the chap who could throw 6-inch nails better than some people could throw darts. Lee Walker of Gravesend, Kent, does just that. On September 9, 1984, in a seven-hour, non-stop marathon stint, Lee struck 4,746 six-inch nails in a dartboard, achieving a total score of 58,609. The total weight of the nails thrown was 3 cwt 3 lb. BOAR

Dominoes

Course
303,621. A new solo record for constructing a domino course, with 303,621 dominoes, was established at the Singapore Expo on August 16, 2003 by Ma Li Hua of China, who for one and a half months, spent 13 hours a day building the giant display. Disaster almost struck during preparations when cock-

Ed Byrne

41-year-old male.
St. Columb, Cornwall, UK.
Married with six children.
Professional martial arts instructor, martial arts
school owner, professional brick breaker.
Web: www.edbyrne.co.uk
E-Mail: masteredbyrne@edbyrne.co.uk
edbyrnepsk@aol.com

7 Karate Chop World Records. Among them:

Broke 24 blocks (2 stacks of 12): Simultaneously

Broke 55 blocks (10 stacks of 1 through 10 blocks): 4.86 seconds

Broke 80 blocks (10 stacks of 8 blocks): 5.75 seconds

Broke 100 blocks (10 stacks of 10 blocks): 10.47 seconds

Broke 120 blocks (12 stacks of 10 blocks): 12.52 seconds

Ed Byrne started breaking concrete blocks at the age of 23, and broke 16 consecutive world records over 17 years. He has also been a world breaking champion since 1992. As a result, he appeared on the front cover of the world's best martial arts magazine, *Martial Arts Illustrated*, broke world records on two martial arts super shows, *The Clash of the Titans*, *The Paul O'Grady Show*, and a documentary on ITV1, *Superhuman: Strong*. Ed has also appeared all over the UK, performing breaking seminars/workshops.

Ed has been invited to compete at the US Open, where he intends to enter and win the World Breaking Championships. He will enter the over 40 years of age and the light-heavy weight division in the power concrete section. Ed is also recognized as being the most successful and influential martial arts coach to come out of the southwest of England, producing 200 Cornish champions, 120 British champions, 6 European champions, and 4 world champions. In 2006, Ed was awarded Instructor of the Year and was voted Coach of the Year at the prestigious Restormel Sports Awards for 2006–2007. His success has continued as his martial arts school has just won the Junior Club of the Year. This year has seen Ed being invited into schools to show students how martial arts and breaking can improve focus and positive mental attitude!

roaches scrambled across the display, toppling more than 20,000 dominoes. BOAR

Stacking
1,001. Matthias Aisch. BOAR

Toppling
4,345,027. Robin Paul Weijers (team leader). BOAR

Duckpin Bowling

Men's Singles
Single game: 279. Pete Signore, Jr.

Three-game set: 655. Jeff Pyles.

Four-game set: 758. Nappy Ranazzo.

Five-game set: 988. William Schwartz.

Six-game set: 1,116. James Deviers.

Seven-game set: 1,329. Jeff Pyles.

Eight-game set: 1,412. Jeff Pyles.

Nine-game set: 1,535. Steve Iavarone.

Ten-game set: 1,760. Jeffrey Ferrand.

Twelve-game set: 2,066. Scott Wolgamuth.

Fifteen-game set: 2,482. Charles "Buddy" Creamer.

Twenty-game set: 3,170. Jeff Pyles.

Twenty-five-game set: 4,028. Jeff Pyles.

Thirty-game set: 4,835. Jeff Pyles.

Season average: 164.47. Jeff Pyles.

Men's Doubles
Single game: 428. J. Lepine and P. Grohs.

Single game: 428. M. Nicholson and C. Plumley.

Three-game set: 1,090. J. Foard and M. Lewinski.

Four-game set:. 1,359. D. Marsh and J. Smith.

Five-game set: 1,739. J. Crunkleton and J. Ferrand.

Six-game set: 1,661. M. Phillips and A. Izzo, Jr.

Season average: 296.66. T. Martin and R. Cochefski.

Men's Triples
Single game: 605. L. Beausoeil, R. Lane, and S. Rodowicz.

Three-game set: 1,548. R. Grant, J. Hayes, and J. Pyles.

Season average: 436. J. Conner, S. St. Clair, and R. Long.

Men's Team of Four
Single game: 763. K. Mumau, J. Howe, J. Vest, and J. Ignatavicius.

Three-game set: 1,974. C. Trilli, R. King, D. Brown, and K. Eastman.

Men's Team of Five
Single game: 909. M. Richburg, J. White, R. Dasch, J. Williams, and M. Steinert.

Three-game set: 2,531. R. Davis Jr., K. Hoffman, D. Huffman, N. Ranazzo, and M. Ogle.

Season average: 725.52. M. Steinert, W. Blizzard Jr., B. Soukup, R. Fullwood, and J. Brady.

Women's Singles
Single game: 265. Carole Gittings.

Three-game set: 586. Diane Jasper.

Four-game set: 741. Amy Bisson.

Five-game set: 877. Amy Bisson.

Six-game set: 1,006. Amy Bisson.

Seven-game set: 1,173. Amy Bisson.

Eight-game set: 1,360. Amy Bisson.

Nine-game set: 1,421. Pat Malthan.

Ten-game set: 1,508. Kathy Spindler-Lischio.

Twelve-game set: 1,806. Veronica Schwarzkopf.

Fifteen-game set: 2,310. Patricia Rinaldi.

Twenty-game set: 2,860. Theresa Vermillion.

Twenty-five-game set: 3,537. Theresa Vermillion.

Thirty-game set: 4,204. Theresa Vermillion.

Season average: 155.08. Amy Bisson.

Women's Doubles
Single game: 374. C. Labulis-Deveglia and S. Thomas.

Three-game set: 1,025. T. Norton and M. Muscillo.

Five-game set: 1,475. A. Rothman and J. Tull.

Season average: 279.03. D. Stevens and E. Williams.

Women's Triples
Single game: 517. K. Fitzwater, C. Celli, and K. Williams.

Three-game set: 1,391. M. Garner, E. Williams, and C. Reynolds.

Women's Team of Four
Single game: 676. D. Shipley, J. Rickels, D. Brenner, and K. Ogle.

Three-game set: 1,829. M. Ritter, D. Pyles, B. Byrum, and C. Byrd.

Women's Team of Five
Single game: 807. E. Williams, E. Bell, M. Mintz, J. Garner, and D. Jasper.

Three-game set: 2,241. J. Stuntz, M. Mintz, J. Garner, E. Bell, and D. Jasper.

Season average: 679. B. Conner, E. Bell, J. Garner, J. Stuntz, and D. Jasper.

Mixed Doubles
Single game: 421. S. Parker and H. James.

Three-game set: 1,040. J. Adams and J. Pyles.

Four-game set: 1,325. T. Pearson and R. Johnson.

Five-game set: 1,658. A. Rothman and J. Crunkleton.

Six-game set: 1,786. C. Bove and J. Bernarding.

Twelve-game set: 3,533. A. Rothman and B. Dawson.

Fifteen-game set: 4,254. C. Gittings and M. Alford.

Season average: 33.626. P. Rinaldi and S. Wolgamuth.

Mixed Triples
Single game: 566. A. Pini, J. Sylvester, and B. Sylvester.

Three-game set: 1,488. F. Guglietti, R. Orts, and P. Rigoulot.

Four-game set: 1,723. J. Baker, D. Grizzard, and S. Hardee.

Mixed Team of Four
Single game: 719. D. Brenner, J. Rickles, R. Dasch, A. Lane.

Three-game set: 1,837. P. Malthan, C. Leonard, J. Johnson, and C. Rhinehart.

Mixed Team of Five
Single game: 842. R. Clayton, J. Foard, T. Hoffman, J. Sala, and T. Hinchliffe.

Three-game set: 2,242. D. Dove, B. Hess, S. Laird, H. Izdebski, and M. Ogle.

Most Number of Games by an Individual
Single season: 1,344. Mariellen Vogt.

Figure Skating

Pirouette
Longest: 3 minutes, 32 seconds. Nathalie Krieg of Switzerland, holds the record for the longest pirouette. For a television show in Erfurt, Germany, on October 11, 1992, Nathalie set a record with a time of 3 minutes, 32 seconds for the longest pirouette.

She said afterward she stopped the record attempt early because she was afraid it would become too boring for the television viewers. BOAR

Golf

Golf Ball Blowing
Distance: 7 feet 2 inches. Ralf Laue. Ball rolled along the floor. BOAR

Golf Ball Spitting
Distance: 18 feet 6¾ inches. Brian Jackson. Ball expelled from mouth. BOAR

Holes Played
12 hours: 15 rounds 6 holes. The most holes played within 12 hours is 276, by Phillip Queller of the USA. Played at the Sky Links Golf Course, Riverside, California, USA, on June 4, 2001. Phillip played without the use of any golf carts or help of any kind. During the 12 hours, he made a total of 1,141 strokes, played 15 rounds 6 holes, covering over 30 miles of play and scored a 17.4 average over par per round. He lost 5 golf balls during the day and wore out 8 pairs of golf gloves. BOAR

Longest Drive
282 yards. Cristian Sterning of Sweden, set the record for the longest single-handed drive with a carry of 282 yards at St. Andrews as part of the Charity World Record Golf Day on June 18, 2005. On the same occasion, Ian Cahill of England caught a golf ball 200 yards from the tee. The ball was hit by Phil Naylor—a new record for the longest golf shot caught. BOAR

photo by Rich Hardcastle

Tim Fitzhigham

31-year-old male.
Derbyshire, Hertfordshire and London, UK.
Single.
Multi-award winning comedian,
shenaniganist, explorer, writer and author,
internationally renowned after-dinner speaker.
Web: www.fitzhigham.com
E-mail: tim@fitzhigham.com

World Records:

Fastest English Channel crossing in bathtub:
9 hours, 6 minutes

Kayaked paper boat 160 miles down the
Thames River

Tim Fitzhigham started as a nutmeg, mace and cocoa farmer in Grenada, West Indies; each evening he'd tell stories to make people laugh in a rum shop down on a goat track. Farming accidentally led to various awards in comedy and radio and TV shows. This led to film, writing columns in newspapers, and touring all over the world doing live shows. These shows (dreamy flights of epic romantic impracticality) were kindly made Critic's Choice in a variety of newspapers.

In 2003, Tim was made a Freeman of the City of London. In 2004, he was made Honorary Freeman of the prestigious Company of Waterman and Lighterman of the River Thames and his paper boat went on display at the National Maritime Museum of Great Britain. In 2005, he was made Waterman to the Unitary Authority of Swindon, given the ancient Yorkshire title of Pittancer of Selby in the Ridings and made Commodore of Sudbury Town Quay in Suffolk. This was also the year he was presented to HM Queen Elizabeth II. The year 2006 saw his bath join the paper boat in the National Maritime Museum, and in 2007, Tim ran up Vesuvius and was made a Fellow of the Royal Geographical Society.

Gum Boot Throwing

Furthest
65.34 meters. The rather unusual sport of gum boot throwing is said to have started in the 1910s in the Finnish countryside. In 1998, the International Boot-throwing Association (IBTA) was founded, which organizes national and international championships. The world record holder is Jouni Viljanen of Finland, who tossed a gum boot 65.34 meters at Kokemäki on May 22, 1999. BOAR

High-wire Walking

Fastest
1,000 meters in 11 minutes, 22.49 seconds. Abudusataer Wujiabudula of China, won the 1,000 meter high-wire walking contest at the 1st World High-wire Championship in Seoul, South Korea. It took 11:22.49 to cross the Han River on a 30 millimeter thick high-wire. BOAR

Hopping

Mile
Fastest: 29 minutes, 11.4 seconds. Tony Murray.

One-legged
100 meters: Fastest: 15.57 seconds. 18-year-old Rommel Griffith set the record for the fastest one-legged hopping over 100 meters. At the Barbados World Records Festival, he hopped a distance in 15.57 seconds on March 31, 2007. BOAR

Hula-hoop

3 revolutions: 82. Lori Lynn Lomeli.

Running
100 meters: Fastest: 14.84 seconds. Roman Schedler of Austria, ran 328 feet (100 m) while spinning a hoop in a time of 13.84 seconds on July 16, 1994. BOAR

1 mile: 7 minutes, 47 seconds. Paul Blair of the USA, ran 1 mile while spinning a hoop in 7 minutes, 47 seconds. He also walked 10 kilometers whilst spinning a hoop in a time of 1 hour, 6 minutes, 35 seconds. BOAR

Tractor Tire Spinning Longest
71 seconds. Roman Schedler of Austria, spun a tractor tire weighing 53 lb. (24 kg) for 71 seconds at the 5th Saxonia Record Festival on September 24, 2000 in Bregenz, Austria. BOAR

In-Line Skating

Pulled Behind a Car
Speed: 191 mph. The fastest anyone has been pulled behind a car (a Porsche sports car) while wearing in-line skates is 191 mph (307.4 km/h). Dirk Auer of Germany, used specially constructed in-line skates for the record attempt. BOAR

Pulled Behind a Motorcycle
Speed: 181.3 mph. The fastest anyone has been pulled behind a motorcycle while wearing in-line skates is 181.3 mph (291.8 km/h). Dirk Auer of Germany, used specially constructed in-line skates for the record attempt and set the record on August 11, 2002, near Darmstadt, Germany. BOAR

Joggling

10 Kilometers
Fastest: 36 minutes, 27 seconds. Michal Kapral of

Canada, ran 10 kilometers while juggling three balls in 36 minutes, 27 seconds at the Longboat Toronto Island Run on September 10, 2006. BOAR

26.2 Miles
Fastest: 2 hours, 57 minutes, 52.2 seconds. Michal Kapral of Canada, ran a full marathon while juggling three balls. This record was established at the Toronto Waterfront Marathon on September 24, 2006. BOAR

Karate

Continuous Full Contact Rounds
7 days: 203. Paddy Doyle.

Most Rounds Fought
6,316. Paddy Doyle between February 1993 and April 2009.

Karate Chopping

Concrete Block
35 x 6 x 2 inches, weighing 54 lb. with 1 x 4 inch spacers. Ed Byrne.

9 blocks (1 stack): Hand Speed: 6 meters/second with a force in excess of 200 kilograms. Ed Byrne.

24 blocks (2 stacks of 12 blocks): Simultaneously. Ed Byrne.

55 blocks (10 stacks of anywhere from 1 through 10 blocks): 4.86 seconds. Ed Byrne.

80 blocks (10 stacks of 8 blocks): 5.75 seconds. Ed Byrne.

100 blocks (10 stacks of 10 blocks): 10.47 seconds. Ed Byrne.

120 blocks (12 stacks of 10 blocks): 12.52 seconds. Ed Byrne.

Kumite

Kumite titles: 9. Paddy Doyle.

Kumite challenge: 110 full contact rounds: 3 hours, 6 minutes. Paddy Doyle.

Rounds fought: 5 hours: 141. Paddy Doyle.

Rounds fought: 1 year: 4,006. Paddy Doyle.

Ladder Walking

Distance: 120.05 feet (36.60 m), Jonathan the Jester. Venue: Muncaster Castle on May 22, 2007.

Leapfrogging

8 Hours
Distance: 17 miles 342 yards. On July 19, 1974, Mike Barwell and Wally Adams from East Yorkshire, United Kingdom, leapfrogged a distance of 17 miles 342 yards (27.4 km) in 8 hours, averaging one leap every five yards, along the disused railway line between Sutton and Hornsea, Humberside, United Kingdom. BOAR

Leg Irons

1 Mile
Fastest: 18 minutes, 34 seconds. Cynthia Morrison aka "The Great Cindini," ran 1 mile wearing leg irons with a 16-inch chain between each shackle. December 22, 2006 in West Palm Beach, Florida.

5 Mile Walk
2 hours, 22 minutes. On December 27, 2006, Cynthia Morrison aka "The Great Cindini," walked the perimeter of The Old Jail in St. Augustine, FL for 16.92 laps, totaling 5 miles, in a time of 2 hours, 22 minutes, wearing leg irons with a 16-inch chain between each leg cuff.

Fastest 100-yard Sprint
57.81 seconds. Cynthia Morrison aka "The Great Cindini," sprinted 100 yards wearing leg irons with a 16-inch chain between each shackle. December 22, 2006 in West Palm Beach, Florida.

Furthest Standing Long Jump
6 feet 2½ inches. Cynthia Morrison aka "The Great Cindini," performed a standing long jump wearing leg irons with a 16-inch chain between each shackle. December 22, 2006 in West Palm Beach, Florida.

Martial Arts

Full Contact Kicks
1 hour: 5,750. Paddy Doyle.

Full Contact Punch Strikes
5 minutes: 2,128. Paddy Doyle.

15 minutes: 7,668. Paddy Doyle.

1 hour: 29,850. Paddy Doyle.

Full Contact Straight-Arm Punches
5 hours: 107,602 strikes. Paddy Doyle.

Uppercuts

1 minute: 586. Paddy Doyle.

Matchstick Throwing

Distance
111 feet. The greatest distance a matchstick has been thrown, without wind assistance, is 111 feet (34 m), achieved by Uwe Hohn of Germany. BOAR

Mobile Phone Throwing

With Battery
Furthest: 311 feet 7 inches. Mikko Lampi of Finland, threw a mobile phone a distance of 311 feet 7 inches (94.97 m) at the 6th Mobile Phone Throwing World Championship in Savonnlina, Finland on August 27, 2005. BOAR

Without Battery
Furthest: 83.32 meters. The alternative world championship, organized by the International Association of Mobile Phone Throwers (where the phones are thrown without batteries) had two world records set on September 8, 2007 in Bischofswerda, Germany: Marko Hübenbecker of Germany, achieved a distance of 83.32 meters and Antje Barthel of Germany threw her phone a distance of 46.01 meters. BOAR

Motorcycling

Circumnavigating Earth
19 days, 8 hours, 25 minutes. Between May 11 and June 22, 2002, Kevin Sanders and his wife, Julia (as passenger), circumnavigated the world on a motorcycle, a distance of 19,461 miles (31,319 km) in a time of 19 days, 8 hours, 25 minutes. BOAR

photo by Roger Donovan

Captain Beany from Planet Beanus
AKA Barry Kirk

54-year-old male.
Port Talbot, Wales, UK.
Single.
Superhero!
Web: www.captainbeany.com
E-mail: captainbeany@hotmail.co.uk

3 World Records:

100 hour bath of baked beans:
September 11–14, 1986

Conveyance of large inflatable baked bean can
26 miles (Flora London Marathon 2007)

Conveyance of plate of baked beans on toast
for 26 miles (Flora London Marathon 2008)

After a charity fund-raiser, Barry Kirk of
Port Talbot, South Wales, United Kingdom,
performed his epic 100-hour, charitable baked
bean bath record attempt, penned the "Bean-a-
thon," at the Aberavon Beach Hotel, September

11–14, 1986. Barry Kirk then amazingly changed his name in May 1991, via deed poll, to that of his wackily created alter ego, the eccentric Captain Beany. To date, Captain Beany from Planet Beanus has extensively traveled around the planet, strutting his stuff in his orange caped-crusading superhero costume, complete with genuine British passport, to extol his wonderfully weird, bizarre and wacky demeanor. His mission on planet Earth is to campaign and promote charitable fund-raising causes for and on behalf of "human beans" for the "beanifit" of mankind!

He has recently converted his third floor apartment into the world's first visual Baked Bean Museum of Excellence in Port Talbot! This orange-hued concoction of haricot heavenly delights contains baked bean cans, promotional mugs, die-cast vehicles, Boston baked bean pots, advertisement literature, etc. He is also the sole leading apolitical campaigning political leader of the New Millennium Bean Party in the United Kingdom. His manifesto is to allow everyone to indulge in a baked bean feast everyday and let off wind now and again! To date, Captain Beany has now "bean" officially recognized by the Eccentric Club in London for his off-beat record escapades and services towards both charity and fund-raising endeavors with the national accolade of "Great British Eccentric First Prize 2009 Award Winner" on April 1, 2009.

Palm Block Strikes

Left Arm
56. Time: 30 seconds. Paddy Doyle.

Right Arm
60. Time: 30 seconds. Paddy Doyle.

Paper Boat

Kayak
Thames river. 160 miles. Tim Fitzhigham kayaked 160 miles down the Thames River in a paper boat using paper paddles. Note: This is the world's oldest maritime record, originally set in 1619 at 40 miles.

Paper Plate

Throwing
Distance: 50 feet 8 inches. On August 10, 1990, Alan Thomas of Yeovil, Somerset, United Kingdom, set a new world record for paper plate throwing when he achieved a distance of 50 feet 8 inches (15.48 m) without wind assistance. BOAR

Parachute Jumps

24 Hours
640. Jay Stokes. This record involved the coordinated efforts of 125 volunteers working in 20-person crews for 4-hour shifts with 3 turbine-powered airplanes. The average time per jump was 2 minutes, 15 seconds. The fastest time for one jump was 1 minute, 55 seconds, and the most jumps in 1 hour was 30.

Pine Board Breaking

Elbow Strike
Alternating: 1 minute: 36. Kevin Shelley. Kevin broke

thirty-six 1.25 x 8 x 10 inch white pine boards with alternating right and left arm elbow strikes.

Single: 1 minute: 43. Kevin Shelley. Kevin broke forty-three 1 x 12 x 12 inch white pine boards with right arm elbow strikes.

Head Strike
30 seconds: 32. Kevin Shelley. Kevin broke thirty-two 1 x 12 x 12 inch white pine boards with a forehead strike, one board at a time.

Pole Climbing

80-foot Pole
Fastest: 9.61 seconds. The record time for climbing an 80-foot (24.4 m) pole is 9.61 seconds, achieved by Mark Bryden of Australia. BOAR

Pyramid

201 men balanced on 10 motorcycles. Distance: 424 feet. Achieved by the Dare Devils team of the Indian Army Signal Corps. ASIA BOOK OF RECORDS

Roller Skating

1,000 Miles
162 hours, 42 minutes, 30 seconds. It took Mathias Lillge of Germany, exactly 162:42:30 to skate 1,000 miles, from June 5 to 12, 2000 at Altranft. BOAR

Backward
26.2 miles: 1 hour, 43 minute, 29 seconds. Jörn Seifert of Germany, completed the Berlin Marathon in 2005 backward on in-line skates in 1:43:29 on September 23, 2005. BOAR

Limbo Splits
Lowest height: 5.75 inches. Xue Wang. ASIA BOOK OF RECORDS

Rope Skipping

2 hours: 23,344. Jan Skorkovsky. BOAR

3 hours: 33,656. Jan Skorkovsky. BOAR

6 hours: 60,300. Jan Skorkovsky. BOAR

Marathon (26.2 miles): 3 hours, 57 minutes, 42 seconds. Harry Escott. BOAR

Longest Distance
1,264 miles. The longest distance traveled rope skipping is 1,264 miles (2,034 km). This record was achieved in 1963 by Tom Morris of Australia, aged 71, who skipped from Brisbane to Cairns. BOAR

Running

160.24 miles in 24 hours. Suresh Joachim.

240 miles in 48 hours. Suresh Joachim.

Fastest 1 mile run in a swimming pool: 39 minutes, 15.7 seconds. Paul Woodland.

Backward, Male
200 meters. 31.56 seconds. Ronald Wegner. BOAR

800 meters. 2:31.3 minutes. Thomas Dold. BOAR

1,000 meters. 3:20.09 minutes. Thomas Dold. BOAR

3,000 meters. 11:19.98 minutes. Biran Godsey. BOAR

1 mile: 5 minutes, 46.59 seconds. Thomas Dold. BOAR

Backward, Female
200 meters. 38.47 seconds. Isabella Wagner. BOAR

800 meters. 3:50.7 minutes. Marga Dolfi. BOAR

5,000 meters. 24:11.6 minutes. Metzler-Mennenga Kerstin. BOAR

10,000 meters. 51:53.2 minutes. Metzler-Mennenga Kerstin. BOAR

Half-marathon. 2:11:42 hours. Metzler-Mennenga Kerstin. BOAR

Marathon. 4:42:39 hours. Metzler-Mennenga Kerstin. BOAR

Grand National
Without a horse: Fastest: 40 minutes. Peter Regan.

Marathon: Holding Plate of Baked Beans
Fastest: 5 hours, 46 minutes, 25 seconds. Barry "Captain Beany" Kirk. Captain Beany of Port Talbot, Wales, United Kingdom, set an unlikely, wacky record attempt by conveyance of a plate of baked beans on toast during the Flora London Marathon 2008 on Sunday, April 13th. The plate of baked beans on toast was conveyed by either left or right hand and Captain Beany did not "spill the beans" during his epic 26-mile run in 5:46:25.

Treadmill Trek—Beans on Toast-athon

Beans on toast on plate held in one hand while walking on a treadmill. Time: 12 hours. Captain Beany.

Running Waiter

1,000 meters: 2 minutes, 59 seconds. Roger Bourbon.
BOAR

5,000 meters: 17 minutes, 44 seconds. Roger Bourbon.
BOAR

10,000 meters: 36 minutes, 56 seconds. Roger Bourbon.
BOAR

20,000 meters: 1:14:58. Roger Bourbon. BOAR

26.2 miles: 2:47:00. Roger Bourbon. BOAR

Shuttle Run

40 lb. backpack: 30 feet: 1 hour: 901 sprints. Paddy Doyle.

116 lb. coal sac: 82 feet: 1 hour: 149 trips. Paddy Doyle.

117 lb. coal sac: 82 feet: 30 minutes: 117 trips. Fred Burton.

Shuttlecock

Controlled with Feet
1 shuttlecock juggled. Time: 4 hours, 37 minutes. Li Huifeng. ASIA BOOK OF RECORDS

Skateboarding

Highest Height Off Ramp
Height: 23.5 feet. Danny Way.

Longest Jump
Distance: 79 feet. Danny Way.

Skiing

Backward Somersaults
31. Freestyle-skier Frederick Eiter of Austria, did 31 backward somersaults on skis on April 28, 2007 at the Pitztaler Gletscher, Austria. BOAR

Both Sides of the Atlantic Ocean
1 day. Oliver Kern. Tyrol, Austria and Denver, CO, USA.

Both Sides of the Pacific Ocean
1 day. Oliver Kern. Naspa Ski Garden, Japan and Snoqualmie, WA, USA and Grouse Mountain, Vancouver, Canada.

Most Lifts
1 day: 52. Oliver Kern. Oliver skied 52 of the Austrian Skiwelt's 90 lifts in 1 day.

Soccer Ball

Balancing on Foot
Longest: 17 minutes, 48 seconds. Manoj Mishra of India, balanced a regulation sized soccer ball on his foot for 17 minutes, 48 seconds on August 15, 2007 in Sainik Nagar, Calcutta, India. BOAR

Balancing on Head
Longest: 16 hours. Manoj Mishra of India, balanced a regulation sized soccer ball on his head for exactly 16 hours without a single break, on January 6, 2006 in Mumbai, India. BOAR

Catching on Back of Hand

Kevin M. Shelley

42-year-old male.
Indianapolis, IN, USA.
Married.
Personal trainer and martial arts instructor
Web: www.headstrike.com
E-mail: ksmartialarts@yahoo.com

4 World Records for Martial Arts
Breaking Demonstrations:

Most pine boards broken with head strikes in 30 seconds: 32

Most pine boards broken with alternating elbow strikes in 1 minute: 36

Most pine boards broken with single elbow strikes in 1 minute: 43

Most toilet lids broken with head strike in 1 minute: 46

Kevin Shelley began martial arts at age 12, in

1979. He instantly took to the more difficult, and sensational aspects, such as weapons training and breaking demonstrations. Breaking with the forehead strike is generally considered to be the most difficult and most dangerous, so it was this that he first set out to master.

In 1999, Kevin broke 31 boards with a forehead strike in 30 seconds on *Guinness World Records™: Primetime*—beating the existing record of 24. He later tied his record on the show *Live with Regis and Kelly*. Recently, on a show in Mexico City, Kevin topped his own record by breaking 32 boards with 3 seconds left on the 30 second clock. Since his first record in 1999, Kevin has appeared on over 100 television shows in over 50 countries, including the US. He has broken other world records, and intends to break and set new records in the future. Both he and his wife enjoy hobbies such as skydiving, rock climbing, cave diving, competitive running, and motorcycling. He works primarily as a personal trainer, but both he and his wife, Ralana, are producing instructional DVDs which will soon be for sale on their Web site, *www.headstrike.com*.

Distance: 78 feet 9 inches. Dean Gould. Brackenbury Sports Center, Felixstowe, United Kingdom on December 11, 2000. Ball kicked by Dave Robinson.

Dribbling
12 cones: 6.56 feet (2 m) apart: Fastest: 19.96 seconds. Martin Jennings.

Heading
30 seconds: 173. Jacek Roszkowski.

Doubles Passing: 11,111 times. Agim Agushi and Bujar Ajeti of Kosovo, headed a soccer ball 11,111 times in 3:55:20 on November 9, 2003 in Starnberg, Germany. BOAR

Running up and down stairs: 1 hour, 12 minutes, 41 seconds. Agim Agushi of Kosovo, walked upstairs 1,920 steps and walked downstairs 1,860 steps in 1:12:41 on August 2, 2002 in the PTK Building in Prishtina. BOAR

Sitting Position: 4:02:01. Agim Agushi of Kosovo, on August 14, 2005 in Flensburg, Germany. BOAR

Walking: Distance: 9 miles 857 yards. Agim Agushi of Kosovo, covered 9 miles 857 yards (15.356 km) in 3:12:39 on October 27, 2002 in Munich, Germany. BOAR

While being driven in a car: 4.34 miles (7 km). Agim Agushi of Kosovo, 7 km on August 17, 2004 in Antalya, Turkey. BOAR

Juggling
Feet and head: Running up and down stairs: 1 hour, 19 minutes. Abraham Munoz of the USA, walked up

and down 2,754 steps in 1 hour, 19 minutes on December 28, 2002 in Morelia Micho. BOAR

Feet, thighs, head, and chest. Most touches: 20,000. Time: 3 hours. Manoj Ahibhusel. Venue: Shivaji Stadium on April 6, 2005. ASIA BOOK OF RECORDS

Control in a sitting position: 4 hours, 30 minutes, 43 seconds. Kenneth Yoga: 4:30:43 on May 26, 2006.

Keeping Up
Running 100 meters while keeping up a soccer ball: Manfred Wagner: 15.9 seconds on July 14, 1996 at the 2nd Rekord-Klub Saxonia Record Festival in Flensburg. BOAR

Running 200 meters while keeping up a soccer ball: 40.26 seconds. Abraham Munoz of the USA, on October 29, 2000 at Wheaton College in Illinois, USA. BOAR

Running 1,000 meters while keeping up a soccer ball: Josef Lochman: 5 minutes, 3 seconds in 1986. BOAR

5,000 meters: 32 minutes, 52 seconds. Krishnan Kumaravelu, ran 5,000 meters while keeping up a soccer ball in 32 minute, 52 seconds on February 26, 2006. BOAR

Running 1 hour: 5 miles 693 yards. Josef Lochman ran for 1 hour while keeping up a soccer ball and covered a distance of 5 miles 693 yards (8,680 m) in 1986. BOAR

Running 26.2 miles: 7 hours, 18 minutes, 55 seconds. Running a marathon while keeping up a soccer ball: Dr. Jan Skorkovský covered 26 miles 385 yards (42.195 km) for the Prague City Marathon on July 8, 1990 in 7:18:55. BOAR

Kicking
2 minutes: 142 passes. Robert Smith.

Penalty Kick
Speed: 72 mph. Dave Robinson.

Spinning
One finger: 4 minutes, 21 seconds. Raphael Harris. The record for spinning a soccer ball on one finger is 4 minutes, 21 seconds, established by Raphael Harris of Israel, on October 27, 2000 in Neve Yacov, Jerusalem. BOAR

Three fingers: 10.6 seconds. The record for spinning 3 soccer balls at the same time is 10.6 seconds, established by Raphael Harris of Israel, on October 27, 2000 in Neve Yacov, Jerusalem—one on the right index finger, one on the left index finger, and one on a mouth stick—for 10.6 seconds. BOAR

Soccer Match

Longest
Time: 40 hours. Players from the Licenced Trade League. No less than 7 players a side played. This applies with FIFA rules. Ross Wishart, Brendan Coyle, Liam Smith, Scott Smith, Joe Ward, James Shiplee, Kieran Hills, Sam Burnside, Nathan Bird, Danny Riseborough, Martin Coad, Richard Sadler, Darren Rodgers, Matt Thompson, Moh Haider, Daniel Flack, Darren Doherty, Adam Boughey, Sean Calver, Dan Middleditch, Jason Middleditch, Scott Ramsey, Sam Bright, Gavin Williams, Ollie Box, Rob Gillan, Sam Dowers, Daniel Prentice, Chris Simcock, Rob Cook, Daniel Ablitt, Daryle Knight, Gideon Shawyer, and Chris Groves.

Softball

Longest Marathon
30 hours, 31 minutes. Brian Edgcomb.

Space Hopping

100 Meters
Fastest: 28.5 seconds. The fastest time to cover 100 meters on a space hopper is 28.5 seconds by 11-year-old Tony Smythe of Stretchford, Birmingham, United Kingdom, at the Birmingham Students Carnival on November 16, 1985. BOAR

Height Jumped
30 inches. The greatest height ever cleared on a space hopper is one of 30 inches, by Janina Pulaski on BBC TV on May 26, 1975. BOAR

Long Jump
Distance: 6 feet 7 inches. A new space hopper long jump record of 6 feet 7 inches (2 m) was set by Vincent Straker, 12, of Peterborough, Cambridgeshire, United Kingdom, on May 27, 1990. BOAR

Spitting

Cherry Stone
Furthest: 88.97 feet. Serge Fougère of France, spat a cherry stone a distance of 88.97 feet (27.12 m). BOAR

Prune Stone
Furthest: 43.14 feet. Serge Fougère of France, spat a prune stone a distance of 43.14 feet (13.15 m). BOAR

Split

Side Position

Longest held: 36 seconds. Jewgenij Kuschnow of Austria, held a side split position—elevated and only supported under both feet—for 36 seconds at the Impossibility Challenger Games in Dachau, Germany on March 30, 2008. BOAR

Stair Climbing

On Hands

787 steps. Ex-circus performer Nikolai Novikov walked downstairs using only his hands when he "walked" down 32 flights of stairs (787 steps) in June 2004. A couple of times the daredevil fell, but luckily his team of doctors followed closely behind to pick him up. Nikolai, from Russia, has practiced handstands since he was 4 years old, and starved himself for 2 days in preparation for the stunt. BOAR

Swimming

Distance

2,500 miles. Martin Strel of Slovenia, accomplished the longest distance ever swam when he completed an approximate 2,500 miles (more than 4,000 km) descent of the Yangtze River from June 10 to July 30, 2004. BOAR

Flow Channel

16 hours, 11 minutes, 18 seconds. Michael Wolfschlucker of Austria. Michael swam in a flow channel with a constant velocity, equivalent to swimming 100 meters in two minutes, for 16 hours, 11 minutes, 18 seconds. BOAR

Foot in Mouth

Distance: ½ mile. Lucky Meisenheimer, M.D., swam ½ mile with his left foot in his mouth in a time of 30 minutes, 14 seconds. This feat took place on March 28, 1979 and was honored with a cartoon by Ripley's Believe it or Not!

Hands and Feet Tied
50 yards: 1 minute, 6 seconds. Set by Tom Morris. BOAR

100 yards: 2 minutes, 22.2 seconds. Set by Tom Morris. BOAR

200 yards: 8 minutes, 15 seconds. Set by Tom Morris. BOAR

7.4 miles (12 km): Fastest: 3 hours, 15 minutes. Henry Kuprashvili.

Open-Water Lake Swim
100 kilometers: 50 swimmer relay: Fastest: 37 hours, 6 minutes. Starting September 13, 2008 at 6:00 a.m. and ending September 14, 2008 at 7:06 p.m. World record set by a 50-swimmer relay team, each individual swimming 2,000 meters on open-water Lake Cane in Orlando, Florida. The record is shared by Mike Marino, Tom Noonan, Skip Yonchik, Andrea Ugazio, Fred Ehmke, Rick Stafford, Mark Weeks, John Keen, Larry Peck, Scott Neumann, Mel Nash, Curtis Wagner, Kevin Anderson, Ben Ohe, Christopher Ohe, George Mann, Walter Caldwell, Tom Knapp, Bruce Atlee, Walter Diloreto, Chris Gaw, Cleve Cooney, Chris Bolfing, David Tattersall, Trung Lively, Frank Wan, Mike Koenig, Chuck Tanner, Jerry Krannebitter, Chris Scott, Hector Torres, James Hunter, Michael Napoli, Mark Myers, Gene Augustin, Joe Moletteire, Joe Furstace, Mark Dickie, Danny Ellis, Rolando Davis, Chris Iselin, Carlos Figueiredo,

Jay Stokes

51-year-old male.
Yuma, AZ, USA.
Married with three sons and one granddaughter.
Professional skydiving instructor,
retired US Army Special Forces—Green Beret.
Web: www.certificationunlimited.com
E-mail: mostjumps@aol.com

5 World Records for Most Parachute Jumps in 24 Hours:

331 jumps in 1995

384 jumps in 1997

476 jumps in 1999

534 jumps in 2003

640 jumps in 2006

Jay Stokes started jumping after joining the US Army in 1974, and just kept going. He got started with civilian skydiving in 1978 and quickly got into competition and training others to jump. Jay completed 24 years of active federal service with the Special Forces and retired honorably as a Chief Warrant Officer 4 in February 1998. After his retirement, Jay did not slow down. He started his own business, training other people as instructors for various types of skydiving disciplines and may set a record for number of students and/or candidates trained by a single person. Jay's greatest accomplishment was raising $40,000 for his two favorite charities: The Special Olympics and the Special Operations Warrior Foundation.

Jay's latest world record of 640 jumps in 24 hours was a major effort that involved coordinating 125 volunteers working in 20 person crews for 4 hour shifts, doing things like packing parachutes, helping him into and out of gear, flying airplanes, etc. They used 3 different turbine-powered airplanes (only one at a time) that were very fast. The average time per jump was 2 minutes, 15 seconds. The fastest time for one jump was 1 minute, 55 seconds, and the most jumps in 1 hour was 30.

Justin Soto, Sean McCormack, Roy McConnell, John Meisenheimer, Lucky Meisenheimer, Alan Lawson, Michael Rogers, Jake Meisenheimer.

Longest: 50.8 miles (82 km). On October 12, 2007, Yuko Matsuzaki set the world record for swimming 50.8 miles (82 km) in an open-water lake swim on Lake Cane in Orlando, Florida.

Table Tennis

Hitting Solo
1 minute: 119 times. David Downes, Jr.

Rally
Longest: 5 hours, 8 minutes. Leif Alexis.

Longest: 5 hours, 8 minutes. Mat Hand.

Tennis

Ball Bouncing
Edge of racquet: 1 minute: 215. The most number of bounces recorded of a tennis ball on the edge of a tennis racquet in 1 minute is 215, by Dean Gould of Felixstowe, Suffolk, of the United Kingdom in June 1999. BOAR

Rally
2 balls: 2,789. On September 26, 1999, Rob Peterson and Ray Miller of the USA, set the record for the longest rally, keeping two tennis balls in play. Both players hit a total of 2,789 shots from the baseline for over 35 minutes. BOAR

24,696. The world's longest rally took place on April 23, 2005 at the Droitwich Spa Lawn Tennis Club at

Droitwich Spa, Worcestershire, United Kingdom, between Steven Worrallo and Allen Benbow of the United Kingdom. They hit 24,696 shots in 7 hours. BOAR

Serves
Consecutive: 8,017. Set by Rob Peterson. BOAR

Three Legged Racing

50 Meters
6.6 seconds. On April 6, 1986, Dirk Lübeck and Thomas Raabe of East Berlin, Germany, set a three-legged racing record for the distance of 50 meters in a time of 6.6 seconds at a sporting event held in Berlin. On the same occasion, Sabine Roos and Gritta Zölfel (also from East Berlin) established the women's record with a time of 8.0 seconds. BOAR

100 Yards
11 seconds. Olympian Harry Hillman, and Lawson Robertson of the USA, hold the record for running the three-legged 100 yard (91.40 m) distance race in a time of 11.0 seconds, in New York on April 24, 1909. BOAR

400 Meters
1 minute, 22.2 seconds. In 1984, Czechoslovakians Emanuel Cerny and Josef Bohman set the world record for three-legged racing 400 meters with a time of 1 minute, 22.2 seconds. BOAR

Most People
30. Distance: 164 feet (50 m). Time: 8.8 seconds. ASIA BOOK OF RECORDS

Toilet Lid Breaking

Head Strike
1 minute: 46. Kevin Shelley. Kevin smashed 46 pine toilet seat lids with his head in 1 minute, one seat at a time.

100 x 10K Relay

Baton Pass
77 hours, 17 minutes, 25 seconds. Florida Striders Track Club. Mike Marino, organizer. Those participating in the race were: Dan Adams, Lisa Adams, Randy Arend, Dave Balz, Stephen Barton, Steve Beard, Jerry Bennett, Libby Bergman, Darin Bickle, David Bonnette, Bob Boyd, Carter Bradford, Lorna Bradford, Christopher Branton, Frank Bronson, Karen Brown, Stephen Brown, Eric Bush, Rushton Callaghan, Bernie Candy, Barbara Carrico, Giselle Carson, Alex Chieu, Vicky Connell, Ellen Crabill, Tim Dalton, CalLee Davenport, Tracy Dawson, Donna Deegan, Tim Deegan, Tareq Farhat, Sebastian Figueroa, Frank Frazier, John Funk, Stephanie Griffith, Mark Grubb, Jerry Grubesky, Gary Hallett, Scott Hershey, Ed Higginbotham, George Hoskins, Kellie Howard, Jim Hughes, Ben Huron, Casey Huron, Anthony Iselborn, Kim Iselborn, Michael Johnson, David Kelley, Ed Kelly, Drew Kenny, Rick Kohn, Ann Krause, Megan Kuehner, Steven Lancaster, Jerry Lawson, Maria Littlejohn, Kim Lundy, Mike Mandt, Andrew Marchand, Mike Marino, Miller McCormick, Christina McDonough, Mike McGinn, Paul McRae, Denise Metzgar, Patty Miller, Shannon Miller, Josh Myers, Tony Nading, Eric Nguyen, Kent Northey, Jonathan Oliff, Matt Parks,

CHAPTER 6

Speed, Skill, and Stamina

Speed, skill, and stamina are the ability to perform tasks fast, with precision, and with no intent to end, respectively. As all human traits, they are subject to inherent skills and training. Everyone has heard the term, "He/she's a natural." Take Tiger Woods for example. As a child he was playing golf and showing the skills and potential to be one of the greatest golf players of all time. Eugene Nagy, a professional pool player, was running consecutive racks of pool balls before finishing high school. His high-run in straight pool was over 400 early in his career. Other people play golf or pool everyday, for hours, throughout their teen and adult lives and never approach the accomplishments of these two natural athletes.

In this section we feature a combination of speed, skill, and stamina records that range from balancing objects, to backpack runs, balloon modeling, knife throwing, beermat flipping (and catching, of course), card cutting, straitjacket escapes, and yo-yo spinning. There's virtually no limit to what the human body can achieve with or without good reason!

Arm Curls

Most in 1 Hour
522. Total weight lifted: 25,264.8 lb. (11,484 kg). Stuart Burrell.

Backpack Run

26.2 Miles
40-lb. backpack: 6 hours, 28 minutes. Paddy Doyle.

50-lb. backpack: 5 hours, 4 minutes (London Marathon). Paddy Doyle.

40-lb. Backpack
½ mile: Indoor treadmill: 2 minutes, 58 seconds. Paddy Doyle.

1 mile: 5 minutes, 35 seconds. Paddy Doyle.

5 km: 20 minutes, 6 seconds. Dustin McClure.

5 miles: Indoor treadmill: 37 minutes, 45 seconds. Paddy Doyle.

10 km: 57 minutes, 2 seconds. Paddy Doyle.

Cross-country speed march: 13 miles. Time: 4 hours, 25 minutes. Paddy Doyle.

15 miles: 2 hours, 35 minutes. Paddy Doyle.

David R. Adamovich
The World's Fastest and
Most Accurate Knife Thrower

62-year-old male.
Freeport, NY, USA.
Married with two children.
Professional knife thrower, minister,
professor of electrocardiography.
Web: www.knifethrower.com
E-mail: throwdini@knifethrower.com

25 World Records as "The Great Throwdini."
Among them:

Most knives thrown around a human target in
1 minute: 144

Fastest time to throw a 10-knife ladder of
death around a human target: 4.0 seconds

Fastest time to throw 10 knives: 3.73 seconds

Most knives thrown within 1 second: 3

Most knives caught in 1 minute: 24

The Rev. Dr. David Adamovich started throwing knives at the age of 50, winning national and world championships in only 5 years. He has been performing as an impalement artist for 8 years. Selected credits include: *Late Night with Conan O'Brien, The Late Show with David Letterman, Stars of the World Famous Moscow State Circus,* ESPN's *Cold Pizza,* Travel Channel's *Magic Road Trip, Good Morning America, Top 100 Guinness World Records™ of All Time, Monday Night Magic,* History Channel's *Modern Marvels,* and *America's Got Talent.*

David appeared in: *A Day on Broadway, The Guinness Book of World Records, Ripley's Expect the Unexpected, American Sideshow, The Daredevil's Manual,* and *Spectacle Circus* magazine. His greatest accomplishment was creating and producing the Off-Broadway show, *Maximum Risk—World Champions on the Edge!* David's created several knife throwing stunts: the Knife-catch, the Double Ladder of Death, and the Card-stab. His act, Maximum Risk—Impalement Arts with a Touch of Magic and Comedy! includes tight and fast throwing of knives, tomahawks and axes around a target girl, throwing blindfolded, speed throwing, throwing through a paper-veil, and the Wheel of Death. A *Ripley's* cartoon features David being the only person to perform the Triple Crown: bullet, arrow, and knife catch. He is the first variety artist to receive magic's highest honor, the coveted Merlin Award by the IMS.

25 miles: 5 hours, 45 minutes. Paddy Doyle.

30 miles: 7 hours, 15 minutes. Paddy Doyle.

42 miles: 9 hours, 57 minutes, 22 seconds. Paddy Doyle.

50 miles: 11 hours, 56 minutes, 22 seconds. Paddy Doyle.

48 hours: Indoor treadmill: 76.02 miles. Mike Buss.

50-lb. Backpack
10 miles: 1 hour, 26 minutes. Paddy Doyle.

Cross-country speed march: 14 miles. Time: 4 hours, 31 minutes. Paddy Doyle.

55-lb. Backpack
Speed march: 40 miles: 14 hours, 50 minutes. Paddy Doyle.

56-lb. Backpack
5 miles: 36 minutes, 49 seconds. Paddy Doyle.

6 miles: 43 minutes, 45 seconds. Paddy Doyle.

Balancing

7-foot Ladder
Chin: 2 minutes, 25.50 seconds. Jonathan the Jester. Venue: Muncaster Castle on May 22, 2007.

Billiard Cue
1 finger (while moving): 589.06 lb. (179.59 m). Alastair Galpin.

Broom
Nose: 2 hours, 1 minute. Leo Bircher of Switzerland.

BOAR

Christmas Tree

Chin: Longest: 56.82 seconds. David Downes aka "Del Lloydo" of Felixstowe, Suffolk, United Kingdom, balanced a 7-foot Christmas tree on his chin during the run up to Christmas in December 2001, for a record-breaking time of 56.82 seconds. BOAR

Golf Ball on Tee

Nose: 34 seconds. On February 3, 2007, Steve Mills balanced a golf ball atop a 2¾-inch tee on his nose for 34 seconds.

Ironing Board

Chin: 3 minutes, 32 seconds. Set On December 9, 2003 at the Henley Road Cricket Stadium, Ipswich, United Kingdom. BOAR

Pencil

Nose: 2 minutes, 33 seconds. Leo Bircher.

Sky Point

Finger: 7-foot object on finger while standing on a walking globe. 14.59 seconds. Jonathan the Jester. Venue: Muncaster Castle on May 22, 2007.

Soccer Ball

Head: 12 hours. Venue: Shree Samartha Vyayam Mandir, Shivaji Park Dadar West, Mumbai, India in January 2006. Manoj Mishra.

Spoon

Nose: Longest: 2 hours, 15 minutes, 40 seconds. Ami Barwell.

Nose: 7. Geoff Amross.

Tatyana Pavlovna Adamovich

65-year-old female.
Bellmore, NY, USA.
Married with one child.
Owner and coach of
Salle Tanya Fencing School, Bellmore, NY.

United States National Champion,
Woman's Foil

Member of the United States Olympic Team,
Munich 1972

Master of Sports, USSR

Junior Champion of Belarus and USSR

Martini and Rossi International Champion
Olympic Golden Rings Award

World record for most fencing lunges in 1
minute: 57

Tatyana Adamovich has a master's degree in
physical education from Adelphi University, is

a graduate of the Belarus Institute of Physical Culture and Sports, and has a degree in sports journalism from the University of Minsk. She taught fencing at C.W. Post and Adelphi universities.

Tatyana received the Olympic Golden Rings Award for her work in developing young, future athletes and Olympians. She began her athletic career in Belarus in track-and-field but then discovered fencing while visiting a sports complex to report for her local radio station. Tatyana found fencing interesting because she felt it was a graceful and highly competitive sport. Her future coach asked if she would like to try it and Tatyana immediately fell in love with the sport. She discovered that she was quite good at it and went on to become Junior Champion of Belarus and the USSR and a candidate for the prestigious Soviet Olympic Team. Tatyana left the USSR after marrying her husband, who is an American citizen. She joined the New York Fencer's Club and trained with the US Olympic Coaches, Michel Alaux and Chaba Eltesh, and was able to qualify for the US Olympic Team.

Balloon

Blowing

Largest: 9 feet. Tim Fitzhigham blew up a 9 foot diameter rubber balloon in 7 hours, 30 minutes with 6,630 breaths.

Most modeling balloons (Qualatex 260) blown at one time: 9. Brian Jackson.

Bursting

1,000: 5 minutes, 33.02 seconds. Gary Gilbert-Anderson and Mike Taylor of Leighton Buzzard, Bedfordshire, burst 1,000 air-filled balloons, held in an 8 x 6 foot container, using only hands, feet, and body on November 18, 1988 at BBC Wood Lane Studio, London, for the Children in Need Appeal. BOAR

Flying

Highest: 21,400 feet. John Ninomya of the USA, broke the record for a flight powered by party balloons. Ninomya floated to a height of 21,400 feet. BOAR

Modeling

Blindfolded: 5 different sculptures (dog, cat, sword, rabbit, and bird in swing): 38.38 seconds. Thomas Blacke.

Dog: Front of body: Fastest: 3.1 seconds (pre-blown balloon). Thomas Blacke.

Dog: Rear of body: Fastest: 4.35 seconds (pre-blown balloon). Thomas Blacke.

100 dogs: 5 minutes, 48 seconds. Ronald van den Berg. BOAR

3 hours: 827. Set by François Cormier of Canada, in 1991. BOAR

6 hours: 1,616. Set by Tip-Top-Till of Germany, in 1999. BOAR

8 hours: 2,269. Tobias Diesner, Markus Kaufmann, and Tobias Schmidt of Germany, made 2,269 balloon flowers (each one from two balloons) within 8 hours at LEGOLAND in Günzburg, Germany. BOAR

10 hours: 2,228. Set by Uwe Lenhardt of Germany, in 1998. BOAR

24 hours: 6,176. Set by Tim "The Balloonatic" of the USA, in 2004. BOAR

Sculpture
Largest: 15,000 square feet. The largest sculpture made from twisted balloons is "Balloon Manor," a 10-room, 15,000 square foot (1,340 m²) "haunted castle" made entirely out of more than 60,000 balloons. The sculpture was designed by Larry Moss of the USA, and constructed in Rochester, New York in October 2005. BOAR

Squeezing
Most people inside. 23. Set by K. Ito. He also holds the record for being inside one himself. Time: 37.1 seconds. ASIA BOOK OF RECORDS

Stuffing
Individual: 37.1 seconds. Ralf Schüler. BOAR

People: 23. Ralf Schüler from Dessau, Germany successfully squeezed 23 people inside a latex balloon. BOAR

Thomas Blacke

42-year-old male.
Johnston, RI, USA.
Married.
Professional magician and escape artist,
author, editor / publisher, consultant.
Web: www.blackemagic.com, www.jedimindtrick.net
www.escapemasters.com
E-mail: blackemagic@aol.com, escapemasters@aol.com

4 World Records as the World's Fastest Magician
and Escape Artist:

Fastest balloon dog from front of body:
3.10 seconds

Fastest balloon dog from behind back:
4.35 seconds

Fastest wrist-strap escape:
1.47 seconds

Balloon sculpting while blindfolded:
5 different sculptures: 39.43 seconds

Thomas Blacke has been performing as a professional magician since the age of 17 in shows that have taken him all over the world. He serves as the International President of Escape Masters—the International Association of Escape Artists, President of the Lulu Hurst Society, Editor/Publisher of *Escape Masters* magazine, and US Vice President of Record Holders Republic—Registry of Official World Records. He holds the degree of Associate of the Inner Magic Circle from the Magic Circle in London, England, and belongs to the world famous Friars Club in NY, the Magic Castle in Hollywood, CA, the International Independent Showmen's Association in Gibsonton, FL, and holds the Commission of Kentucky Colonel.

Thomas' act is a unique combination of magic, escapes, comedy, sideshow, and vaudeville. He has been featured on a number of television programs throughout the world as well as numerous magazines and periodicals. The effects and routines in his show are designed specially for his act, which makes his show certainly a one of a kind entertainment experience. The show includes the world's fastest balloons, the world's fastest escape, as well as routines with Rubik's cubes, nails, animal traps, lollipops, and a straitjacket.

Beer Bottle

Opening
300 bottles: Fastest: 1 hour, 17 minutes, 7 seconds. A team of 3 from the local brewery of the Slovak town of Topol'cany opened 300 beer bottles in 1:17:7 in 2004. Jozef Frano was the team leader of the winning team. BOAR

Beer Glass

Catching
1 pint: 3.06 seconds. Dean Gould. From table to elbow to drop/catch.

Beermat Catching (palm up)

Off Elbow
Blindfolded: 125. Dean Gould.

WORLD CHAMPION TRICK ROPER, CHRIS MCDANIEL SET THE BULLWHIP WORLD RECORD FOR CRACKING 61 TARGETS FROM THE HAND OF AN ASSISTANT IN 1 MINUTE!

artoon by Sean Hopkins

Interlocking wide stack: 2,390. Dean Gould.

Single stack: 402. Dean Gould.

Beermat Catching (palm down)

Off Each Elbow
60 (120 total). Dean Gould.

Off Elbow
107. Dean Gould.

Blindfolded: 52. Adam Gould.

Beermat Flipping

Off Bottle
35. Dean Gould.

Off Chin
42. Dean Gould.

Off Table
112. Mat Hand.

1,000 (25 stacks of 40 each): 45 seconds. Dean Gould.

Blindfolded: 71. Dean Gould.

Each hand: 65 (130 total). Dean Gould.

One-handed: 208 (interlocked in 3 piles). Dean Gould.

Two fingers: 47. Dean Gould.

Two fingers: Blindfolded: 16. Dean Gould.

Bench Press

1 Hour
55,500 lb. James Clark.

Zdenek Bradac

21-year-old male.
Prague, Czech Republic.
Single.
Magician, juggler, world record breaker.
Web: www.zdenekbradac.com
E-mail: zdenekbradac@email.com

Among Zdenek's World Records:

Longest duration juggling 3 Petang globes:
101 minutes

Most juggling catches whilst suspended:
412 catches

Fastest time to arrange a shuffled deck of cards:
36.16 seconds

Longest juggling duration whilst suspended:
2 minutes, 13.22 seconds

Most juggling catches in 1 minute:
336 catches

Zdenek Bradac started making magic at age of 11 and juggling at the age of 13. When he started, no one taught him magic tricks and juggling. At the age of 17, he broke his first Czech national juggling record for the longest juggling duration of floor objects. From that time on, he wished to become a world record breaker. At the age of 19, Zdenek broke his first world record for the longest duration juggling whilst suspended by the knuckles. Then, he was a performer in the prestigious International Record Festival in Pelhrimov and while there, broke two other world records. At the age of 20, Zdenek also broke his first Guinness World Record™ on the TV show *Ripley's Believe It or Not*.

Zdenek holds many current Guinness World Records™. He concentrates especially on juggling and magical records, such as the most juggling catches in 1 minute or the fastest time to re-arrange a shuffled deck of cards. After a few years, his passion for magic, juggling, and records never stopped. Thanks to his records, he is a bit different than most magicians. Now, Zdenek is preparing many new records and illusions at the world level. His hardest records are just coming and he is going to show that very soon in America, too.

110 lb.
30 minutes: 1,107 repetitions. Karl Eugen Reck.

Brick Balance

On Palm, 4.5 lb. Brick
12. Fred Burton.

Brick Carrying

One-Handed, pinch grip: 10 lbs.: 80.37 miles. Paddy Doyle.

Brick Catching

Most times caught from thrower to catcher then catcher to thrower: 25. Time: 1 minute. Dean Gould and Nick Claydon.

Brick Flipping

4.5 lb. Brick
12 bricks consecutively: 11.52 seconds. Dean Gould.

Brick Lift Off Table

One-Handed, 4.5 lb. Brick
15. Fred Burton.

Brick Lift Repetitions

Two Bricks at 4.5 lb. Each, One-Handed
1 minute: 46. Dean Gould.

Card Cutting

Most One-Handed Cuts
1 minute: 57. Matt Cassiere.

One-Handed
"Charlier" double cut: Simultaneous L/R: Fastest

time to complete 30 total cuts (15 each hand, simultaneously): 29.25 seconds. Simon Lovell. Performed September 2006 at Fantasma Magic, NYC, RHR's "World Records of Magic Show."

"Erdnase" triple cut: Fastest time to complete 30 total cuts: 1 minute, 27.56 seconds. Simon Lovell. Performed September 2006 at Fantasma Magic, NYC, RHR's "World Records of Magic Show."

"Simey" quadruple cut: Simultaneous L/R: Fastest time to complete 10 total cuts (5 each hand, simultaneously): 48.34 seconds. Simon Lovell. Performed September 2006 at Fantasma Magic, NYC, RHR's "World Records of Magic Show."

CD Flipping

Most
46. Dean Gould. Felixstowe, United Kingdom on May 23, 2004.

CD Snatching

Off Elbow
54. Dean Gould. Felixstowe, United Kingdom on June 21, 2005.

Chest Passes

Most
5 minutes: 524. Dave Robinson.

Chest Press

1 Minute Total
4,400 lb. (2,000 kg). Dave Robinson.

Stuart Burrell

32-year-old male.
Essex, England.
Single.
E-mail: stuart.burrell@googlemail.com

3 World Records:

Most handcuff escapes in 1 hour: 301

Most arm curls in 1 hour:
522. Total weight lifted: 11,484 kg

Most weight lifted by triceps in 1 hour: 1,088 kg

Stuart Burrell was the classic "geek" at school and was also a bit on the large side. He had no interest in team sports. The only world record that anyone could see in his future was for "Most Bullied." That situation changed once Stuart started going to the gym at the age of 13. Soon, he was competing against some of the very students who had been his harshest critics. Some of them took it well whilst others did not. Then, in 2002 Stuart set a world record in escapology by escaping from 301 handcuffs in 1 hour. That record showed him anything was possible.

A couple of years later, Stuart started to look into the fitness records held with Record Holders Republic and found that some were within his reach. He then set the arm curl and triceps records. Stuart says, "It was an honor to set those records at the gym I started out in. It was my way of saying thank you to the owners for giving me a purpose in life. It also brought everything full circle. The main lesson I have learned through all these record attempts is believe in yourself and you can achieve the unbelievable."

Chin-ups

1 Minute, Female
33. Alicia Weber. BOAR

30 Minutes, Male
493. Stephen Hyland. BOAR

30 Minutes, Female
297. Alicia Weber. BOAR

60 Minutes, Male
908. Stephen Hyland. BOAR

60 Minutes, Female
535. Alicia Weber. BOAR

Clothespins

Picked off Clothesline with One Hand
24. Dean Gould. Felixstowe, United Kingdom on August 1, 2006.

Coin Flicking

Furthest
38 feet. Dean Gould.

Coin Manipulation

One-Handed (Downs Palm)
8 US Silver dollars: 16.75 seconds. Justin Style.

9 US Silver dollars: 17.38 seconds. Justin Style.

10 US Silver dollars: 21.97 seconds. Justin Style.

Simultaneous rolls: US ½ dollar: 8. Richard Turner.

Coin Snatching (from elbow)

1 Pence
374. Dean Gould. Caught palm down. 374 caught, some dropped prior to catch.

2 Pence
212. Dean Gould. Caught palm down, 212 caught, some dropped prior to catch.

10 Pence
100. Dean Gould. Caught palm down, 100 percent clean catch, no drops.

328. Dean Gould. Caught palm down, 328 caught, some dropped prior to catch.

Contortion

Tennis racquet: 3 horizontal passes: 26.23 seconds. Jared Rydelek.

Squash racquet: 3 vertical passes: 23.32 seconds. Jared Rydelek.

Pretzel push-ups: 20: 15.72 seconds. Jared Rydelek.

Cross-Country Skiing Machine

Distance: 1 mile. Time: 6 minutes, 48.04 seconds. Paul Woodland.

Distance: 10 miles. Time: 1 hour, 19 minutes, 12.69 seconds. Paul Woodland.

Time: 30 minutes. Distance: 4.03 miles. Paul Woodland.

Time: 1 hour. Distance: 7.53 miles. Paul Woodland.

Fran Capo
The World's Fastest Talking Female

37-year-old female.
Putnam County, NY, USA.
Divorced with one son.
Comedienne, keynote motivational speaker,
actress, voice-over artist, nine-time author,
TV host, ordained minister, hypnotist, adventurer.
Web: www.FranCapo.com
E-mail: FranCNY@aol.com

3 World Records:

Fastest talking in 1 second:
11 words (603.32 words in 54.2 seconds)

Highest book signing:
19,340 feet, on Mt. Kilimanjaro

Deepest book signing:
12,465 feet below sea level, at the Titanic

In sixth grade, Fran Capo had a teacher who made her nervous, so she talked fast. Kids laughed, and it launched two careers: comedy and fast-talking. Fast forward (pun intended)... She graduated from Queens College then worked at a radio station as sultry weather reporter, June East (Mae West's long lost sister). With her motto of, "Just say yes and figure it out later," Fran broke the fast-talking record on *Larry King Live*. That led to appearances on over 350 television and 2,500 radio shows, including: *Entertainment Tonight, Good Morning America*, Nick at Nite, the Discovery Channel, *The Martha Stewart Show*, and CNN, where her segment was voted top five watched for the week.

Fran writes a weekly blog, "Fran's World," for the WB and has a TV show by the same name on *www.rockmetv.com*. She's written nine books, including: *Adrenaline Adventures* and *Almost a Wise Guy*. Fran does spokesperson work for Fortune 500 companies and travels the world doing wild adventures: race car driving, bungee jumping, swimming with sharks, etc. As long as she's motivating people, making them laugh, staying healthy, and loving her family, she says she's happy. Fran's motto: Live everyday as if it's your last, and one day you'll be right.

Cucumber Snapping

Most
75. Time: 1 minute. Alastair Galpin.

Dancing

Kathak
24 hours, 8 minutes. Payal Mathur. Kathak is an Indian dance that follows a progression in tempo from slow to fast, ending with a dramatic climax.

Macarena
652. Barbara Hannant. 552 children, parents, and staff of the Plumcroft Primary School, UK, performed the Macarena dance, simultaneously.

Oops Upside Your Head
565. Barbara Hannant. 565 children of the Plumcroft Primary School, UK, performed the Oops Upside Your Head dance, simultaneously.

Thriller Dance: Largest Simultaneous (One Location)
903 people: Kimber McDermott. On September 6, 2009, 903 people from DragonCon, Atlanta, GA, simultaneously performed the Thriller dance.

Thriller Dance: Multi-Location
22,596 people: Ines Markelle. On October 25, 2009, at 12:30 a.m., 22,923 people from 32 countries simultaneously danced the Thriller dance as part of the Thrill the World Event. Countries included: Argentina, Australia, Austria, Canada, China, Colombia, Costa Rica, Czech Republic, England, France, Finland, Germany, Ireland, Japan, Malaysia, Mexico, Netherlands, New Zealand, Peru, Poland, Russia, Scotland, Serbia, Singapore, Slovakia, South Korea,

Sweden, Switzerland, Thailand, Turkey, United States of America, and Venezuela.

Domino Snatching

Off Elbow
16. Dean Gould.

Drumming

10 Seconds
220 strokes. Art Verdi.

1 Minute
Strokes: 1,180. Mike Mangini.

Average Double Bass Beats over 10 Minutes
158.9 BPM. The Jerome Experience. Venue: The Bay Tree Public House at Grove, Oxfordshire on July 7, 2007.

Double Bass Marathon with Legs Only
2 hours. Miles each leg: Left: 12.19; Right: 11.15. The Jerome Experience. Venue: The Bay Tree Public House, Grove, Oxfordshire on July 7, 2007.

Fastest Double Bass Drums with Legs Only
163.1 BPM. The Jerome Experience. Venue: The Bay Tree Public House, Grove, Oxfordshire on July 7, 2007.

Feet
Bass roll: Single strokes: 1 minute: 1,057. On September 17, 2006, Tim Waterson of Edmonton, Alberta, Canada, broke his previous world record of 1,030 bass roll strokes at the M&M Studios in Andrew, Alberta, Canada.

Paul Carpenter

31-year-old male.
Houston, TX, USA.
Single.
Professional magician, escape artist,
mentalist, hypnotist, singer, actor.
Web: www.mentallyhyp.com
www.myspace.com/mentallyhyp
E-mail: mentallyhyp@gmail.com

2 World Records:

Fastest standing straightjacket escape:
10.96 seconds

Fastest 6 bends in 10 individual forks:
58.67 seconds

Paul Carpenter has been performing since the age of 6. He started singing and taking vocal training at the age of 8. He fell into the world of magic and illusion by the age of 10, and became very keen on the ability of the mind, beginning to induce subjects at 13. Paul has been featured in television shows and on stages all over the world. Some of these accolades include receiving the fastest straightjacket escape record. He was also a finalist in *In Search of the Partridge Family* beating out over 10,000 people.

Paul has been on national television programs, including: NBC, CBS, Corus network, morning news, and affiliated programs. He was also featured in an Internet commercial spot for *Criss Angel: Mindfreak*. The list certainly goes on and on. Paul has spent the last two years in New York, where he was placed in *Ripley's Believe It or Not!*, had his own successful one-man, Off-Broadway show, and just finished his first in a series of DVDs with Magic Makers, Inc. Paul is now currently traveling to Australia for a national tour of the down under and will be traveling extensively throughout the world as of April 2008.

Longest Marathon
84 hours. Suresh Joachim.

Loudest
115 decibels. The Jerome Experience. Venue: Bay Tree Public House, Grove, Oxfordshire on July 7, 2007.

Ear Wiggling

1 Minute
147. Jitendra Kumar.

Egg Crushing

Head
30 seconds: 20. Alastair Galpin.

Egg Holding

Back of Hand
14. Dean Gould.

Elbow Power Block (speed)

Left Arm
66. Time: 30 seconds. Paddy Doyle.

Right Arm
68. Time: 30 seconds. Paddy Doyle.

Elbow Strikes

Left Arm
54. Time: 30 seconds. Paddy Doyle.

Right Arm
57. Time: 30 seconds. Paddy Doyle.

Elbow to Palm-up Catch

34 lb. Dean Gould.

Endurance Performance

Breath Holding
17 minutes, 4.4 seconds. David Blaine. Performed as "Breath Holding."

Encased
Box of ice: 63 hours, 42 minutes, 15 seconds. David Blaine. Performed as "Frozen in Time."

Entombed
Underground plastic box beneath a 3-ton water-filled tank: 7 days. David Blaine. Performed as "Buried Alive."

Fasting
Water only: 44 days. David Blaine. Performed as "Above the Below."

Spinning
8 revolutions per minute in a gyroscope: 16 hours. David Blaine. Performed as "Revolution."

Standing
105-foot high by 22-inch wide pole: 35 hours. David Blaine. Performed as "Vertigo."

Water Submersion
Full body: 177 hours. David Blaine. Performed as "Drowned Alive."

Endurance Challenges
6: Paddy Doyle

Arden & Warwickshire Cross–Country Challenge
7 hours, 52.23 seconds: 30 miles carrying a 40 lb.

James Clark

43-year-old male.
New Hope, MN, USA
Platonic metaphysics teacher of philosophy,
theology, and Spanish.
E-mail: jamesbclark2004@yahoo.com

9 World Records in Strength and Endurance.
Among them:

Most sit-ups in 24 hours: 44,001

Most weight lifted on a pull down machine: 91,000 lb. in 1 hour

Most sit-ups done in 1 hour with 50 pounds: 1,575

Most sit-ups done in 1 hour: 2,200

Most pull-ups and push-ups done in 1 hour, 17 minutes: 1,001 of each

In 1987, James Clark did 2,001 parallel bar dips in 1 hour. In 1988, he did 33,001 push-ups in 24 hours, and then in 1989, he broke the world record for sit-ups in 24 hours doing 44,001. James was invited to be a guest on *The Late Show with David Letterman*. While on the show, he did 1,534 sit-ups in about 40 minutes. Also in 1989, he broke Jack LaLanne's world record of 1,000 push-ups and 1,000 pull-ups in 1 hour, 22 minutes by doing 1,001 of each in 1 hour, 17 minutes.

After completing his B.A., M.A. and Ph.D. degrees, James returned to weight lifting competition and in 2003, he broke a world record by bench-pressing 25,500 kilos in 1 hour. In 2004, James broke 5 world records in the same day, including performing 1,575 sit-ups in 1 hour while holding a 50 lb. weight on his chest. In 2006, he broke the world record for sit-ups in 1 hour by doing 2,201. James did another sit-up demonstration by doing 121 sit-ups without stopping while holding an extra 75 lb. on his chest. James broke a record on April 19, 2008 in weight lifting by lifting 91,000 lb. in 58 minutes. This feat was performed on a lat pull down machine.

backpack over hills and cross-country in winter conditions. Paddy Doyle.

Endurance Strength Title Record
9 hours, 55 minutes: 833 steps with a 40 lb. backpack on a 15-inch step, 51.47 miles on an indoor Concept Rower (zero resistance), 83 miles on an indoor cycle (zero resistance), 130 back-of-the-hand push-ups with a 40 lb. backpack, and 220 shuttle sprints of 30 feet with a 40 lb. backpack. Paddy Doyle.

Guinness Physical Fitness Challenge Record
18 hours, 56 minutes, 9 seconds: 12 mile run, 12 mile walk carrying 25 lb. backpack, 1,250 push-ups, 1,250 star jumps, 3,250 sit-up crunches, 1,250 standing hip flexors, 110 mile cycle, 20 mile row, 20 miles on cross trainer, weight lifting 300,000 lb., 2 mile swim. Paddy Doyle.

World's Fittest Athlete Record
21 hours, 21 minutes, 2 seconds: 12 fitness challenges. 12 mile walk carrying 25 lb. backpack, 12 mile run, 2 mile swim, 110 mile cycle, weight lifting 312,170 lb., 1,250 press-ups, 1,250 star jumps, 3,250 sit-up crunches, 20,000 meters on rower, 1,250 hip flexor reps with 5 lb. weight, 1 mile run carrying 44 lb. backpack, 3 kilometers on gym stepper. Paddy Doyle.

World Fitness Champion Title Record
17 hours, 12 minutes, 33 seconds: 2 mile 21 meter swim, 20 mile row, 20¼ miles on cross trainer, 10 mile speed march with 25 lb. backpack, 100¾ mile cycle, 550 star jumps, 3,010 sit-up crunches, 300,000 lb. weight lifting, 10¼ mile run, 505 hanging leg lifts. Paddy Doyle.

World Speed Fitness Challenge Record
Six 1-minute events with 1 minute rest intervals between: 123 press-ups, 108 sit-ups, 114 one-armed push-ups, 90 squat thrusts, 33 burpee's, 102 back-of-the-hand push-ups. Paddy Doyle.

Escaping

Handcuffs
Fastest: 2.5 seconds. Cynthia Morrison. September 7, 2006.

Underwater: 3.16 seconds. Cynthia Morrison. September 11, 2006.

Straitjacket
Buried alive under beach sand: 2 minutes, 5 seconds. Cynthia Morrison. Cynthia performs as "The Great Cindini." Cynthia was buried alive from head to toe in a 2-foot deep trench under beach sand in Singer Island, FL, USA, just feet from breaking ocean water.

Fastest female: 14.66 seconds. Cynthia Morrison. Cynthia performs as "The Great Cindini."

Fastest inverted: 19.20 seconds. Cynthia Morrison. Cynthia performs as The Great "Cindini."

Fastest male: 10.94 seconds. Paul Carpenter.

On stilts: 25.37 seconds. Cameron Tomele. Performed on 2.5-foot peg stilts.

Underwater
Straitjacket and chains: Fastest: 34 seconds. Dan Robinson.

With Chains: Fastest: 10.76 seconds. Dan Robinson.

Paddy Doyle
The World's Fittest Endurance Athlete

44-year-old male.
Birmingham, UK.
Single.
Physical fitness coach and qualified
adventure training mountain leader.
Web: www.worldsfittestathlete.co.uk
E-mail: patrick814@btinternet.com

69 World Records. Among them:

Most press-ups in a calendar year:
1,500,230 (averaging 4,000 per day)

1 mile run carrying a 40 lb. backpack:
5 minutes, 35 seconds

Most full contact boxing martial arts rounds
fought: 6, 316

World's fittest athlete:
11 events in 18 hours, 56 minutes

Most one-armed push-ups in 5 hours: 8,794

Paddy Doyle began strength and fitness records in 1987 at the age of 23, performing 4,100 push-ups with a 50 lb. weight on his shoulders in 4 hours, 30 minutes. Since then, Paddy has competed in National Amateur Judo tournaments—winning junior bronze and silver medals. He's represented his school and the army cadets, winning silver and gold medals in cross-country tournaments. Paddy progressed to amateur boxing, fighting at light welter, welter, and light middle weight inter-club competition. Mixing boxing with full contact martial arts, he's won 10 Kumite title records.

Paddy has appeared in 16 editions of *The Guinness Book of World Records*, 5 times on BBC's *Record Breakers*, *Sky News* UK, Irish TV and German TV. He has a dedicated team who trains and supports him in all his competitions and record events. To date, Paddy has amassed a total of 163 records, from the local club level to world records. As a member of the UK Parachute Regiment, he had the opportunity to train paratrooper cadets. Paddy hopes to be an inspiration to all future endurance and sport athletes.

Alastair Galpin

35-year-old male.
Auckland, New Zealand.
Single.
Sustainable housing developer,
professional world record breaker.
Web: www.worldrecordchase.com
E-mail: info@worldrecordchase.com

70 World Records. Among them:

Most rhinestones on body: 31,680

Largest cartoon: 862 square meters

Longest handshake: 9 hours, 19 minutes

Most hugs in 1 hour: 624

Most socks worn on 1 foot: 74

Alastair Galpin began breaking world records in 2004 by suspending weights from his tongue at home. It took several years for his local community to see the goal he was pursuing with acts like that. Now, with some experience, Alastair routinely breaks a wide variety of world records to promote community and conservation organizations. Some challenges are big, such as attempting to cook the largest bowl of soup—25,000 liters—while others are simple activities, like sticking snails all over his face. Says Alastair, "It's a pleasure to travel and tell my tales to school groups, and I sometimes include a world record attempt simply for entertainment."

Of most interest to Alastair is promoting good causes in regions where international media is difficult to attract. Such events take lots of creative thinking and are great to tackle. His work has appeared in most New Zealand media, in *National Geographic Kids*, on ABC, in several editions of *Guinness World Records*™, on Radio Canada International, and has been distributed by Reuters. Each year, Alastair looks forward to overcoming record breaking challenges which will raise awareness for a range of deserving causes. Says Alastair, "This is what makes life worthwhile and it's a great way to keep active!"

Wrist-Strap
Fastest: 1.47 seconds. Thomas Blacke. Performed September 2006, Fantasma Magic, NYC, RHR's "World Records of Magic Show."

Fencing

Lunges: 1 Minute
57. Tatyana Adamovich.

Fork Bending

10 Forks
6 bends each: Fastest: 52.62 seconds. Paul Carpenter. September 2006 at Fantasma Magic, NYC, RHR's "World Records of Magic Show."

Game

Operation
Fastest: 48.6 seconds. Ralf Laue of Germany, completed a game of Operation in the world record time of 48.6 seconds at the Impossibility Challenger Games in Dachau, Germany on March 30, 2008. BOAR

Gift Wrapping

Book
Fastest: 32.7 seconds. Alastair Galpin.

Handball

Ball-Control with Feet
3 hours, 6 minutes, 24 seconds. Haruna Abdulazeez. Haruna kept a handball aloft with the use of only his feet. BOAR

Handstand

One-Armed Push-ups
12. Circus performer Yury Tikhonovich of Russia, performed an impressive 12 push-ups while standing on one hand, in June 2006 at the Starclub variete in Kassel, Germany. He repeats this feat almost everyday in rehearsal for his show. BOAR

Jenga Block Catching

Balanced on Forearm and Caught Palm Up
54. Felixstowe, United Kingdom on May 29, 2006. Dean Gould.

Juggling

Blindfolded
3 balls: 25.31 seconds. Zdenek Bradac. Ball size: 68 mm. Ball weight: 140 grams.

Dean Gould
The World's Most Dexterous Man

43-year-old male.
Felixstowe, Suffolk, UK.
Married with three children.
E-mail: dgould378@aol.com

40 World Records. Among them:

Coin snatching a UK 10 pence balanced on elbow, caught palm down: 328

Catching beermats balanced on elbow, all caught palm up: 2,390

Most number of tennis ball bounces on the edge of a racket in 1 minute: 215

Flipped beermat 180° from the edge of a table, one-handed: 208

Double finish in darts in 36 seconds: 301

Dean Gould started record breaking when he was 20 years old and had so many records by the mid-nineties that he was invited to the World Record Festival in Flensburg, Germany, which is equal to going to the Olympics, only that every participant is a world champion. He has performed at three of the six Flensburg Festivals, which is an achievement in itself.

Being a record breaker has made Dean famous in Felixstowe, Suffolk. He once went out disguised, wearing a Freddie mask (from *Nightmare on Elm Street*), only for someone to say to him, "When are you doing your next record Dean?" His favorite record, and the most difficult to do, is flipping 35 beermats off the top of a lager bottle. He catches all beermats and picks the bottle up at the same time with the same hand. Dean can hold his head up high and say that he is one of the top 10 record breakers in the world and he feels he has made a mark in the history of human achievement. Dean's most significant achievement in the field of world records was to conceive and develop Record Holders Republic. They're now into a second record related book.

3 clubs: 1 minute, 56 seconds. Iryna Bilenka. BOAR

Burning Globes
10.4 seconds. Zdenek Bradac. Three 65-mm, 110-gram burning globes were juggled for 32 throws in 10.4 seconds.

4. Zdenek Bradac. Four 65-mm, 110-gram burning globes were juggled for 11 throws in 3.38 seconds.

Catches
3 balls: 1 minute: 336. Zdenek Bradac. Ball size: 43 mm. Ball weight: 46 grams.

Football
With feet: 35. On March 22, 2007, Paul Nardizzi juggled an American Football from the top of his feet 35 times (using both feet, only one contacting the football at any one time).

Petang Globes (3)
101 minutes: Zdenek Bradac. Globe size: 71 mm. Globe weights: 710 grams, 692 grams, and 718 grams. Total number of throws: 22,119. Total weight thrown: 15,638 kg.

Suspended from Knees
3 balls: 1 minute, 20.13 seconds. Zdenek Bradac. Ball size: 68 mm. Ball weight: 140 grams.

While Hopping
3 objects: 164 feet (50 m): 21.93 seconds. Joel Dickinson. Venue: Muncaster Castle on May 22, 2007.

Knife Throwing

Most Knife Throwing Records
24. David R. Adamovich aka "The Great Throwdini," has set and broken more world records for his knife throwing skills than any other knife thrower in history. All records performed with 14-inch professional throwing knives.

Fastest Double Ladder of Death
16 knives: 6.1 seconds. David R. Adamovich aka "The Great Throwdini." Performed with knife thrower Harry Munroe and Target Girl Tina Nagy. Previously 6.5 seconds with Target Girl Joan Munroe.

Fastest Time to Throw 10 Knives
3.73 seconds. David R. Adamovich aka "The Great Throwdini." Previously 3.97 seconds and 4.27 seconds.

Fastest Time to Throw a 10-knife Ladder of Death Around a Human Target
4.0 seconds. David R. Adamovich aka "The Great Throwdini." Performed with Target Girl Tina. Previously 5.0 seconds.

Fastest Time to Throw a 16-knife Ladder of Death around a Human Target
7.67 seconds. David R. Adamovich aka "The Great Throwdini." Performed with Target Girl Kryssy Kocktail.

Fastest Time to Throw 10 Knives Around a Human Target (1 knife/throw)
4.29 seconds. David R. Adamovich aka "The Great Throwdini." Performed with Target Girl Tina Nagy. Previously 4.98 seconds.

Doug Hunt

51-year-old male.
Brantford, Ontario, Canada.
Married.
Stilt walker, magician, juggler, director of
marketing, fund-raising and volunteer services.
Web: www.Dougthegreat.com
E-mail: Doug@DougtheGreat.com

3 World Records:

Tallest stilts ever mastered:
50 feet 9 inches: 29 steps

Heaviest stilts ever mastered:
137 lb. total: 29 forward steps

Most people to simultaneously walk on stilts:
625, organized by Doug Hunt

Doug Hunt is currently the Director of Fund-raising, Marketing, and Volunteer Services at Participation House Brantford. This is a non-profit organization striving to meet the needs of physically challenged adults living in his community. On September 14, 2002, Doug set the record for the world's tallest stilt-walker, in Brantford, Ontario, Canada, by taking 29 independent and unassisted steps on stilts measuring 50 feet 9 inches and weighing a combined weight of 137 lb. Doug's two stilt-walking world records were set as part of a series of events supporting Participation House Brantford and the clients they serve—"A walk on stilts for those who cannot walk." To date, they have raised over $50,000. These World Records were accomplished after years of work and with the support and encouragement of an extremely dedicated and dynamic team.

Also known as "Doug the Great—Entertainer," Doug is a member of the International Brotherhood of Magicians and the International Jugglers Association. As a child, his interest in magic, juggling, and the performing arts was encouraged by his parents to help him overcome shyness. (It seems to have worked!) Doug's biggest fans and constant supporters are his wife, Katie, and their daughter, Megan.

Fastest Time to Throw 10 Knives into the Wheel of Death
4.80 seconds. David R. Adamovich aka "The Great Throwdini." Ten 14-inch throwing knives were thrown into a revolving Wheel of Death at 2 knives per revolution (1 knife at a time) within 4.8 seconds, as the wheel spun at 1 revolution per second.

Fastest Time to Throw 22 Knives in Ladder of Death
9.87 seconds. David R. Adamovich aka "The Great Throwdini."

Knife Catch: 1 Minute
25. David R. Adamovich aka "The Great Throwdini." Knives thrown 1 full spin by Dick Haines.

Triple Crown: the Bullet Catch, Arrow Catch, and Knife Catch
David R. Adamovich aka "The Great Throwdini." David is the first and only person to have performed all three of the most difficult and dangerous projectile catches.

Most Accurate Impalement Arts Stunt: The Annie Oakley Cigarette Ash Challenge
Knocked 1/4-inch ash off the end of a lit 3¼-inch cigarette held in the mouth of a target girl without touching the cigarette, a distance of 2 inches from her nose. David R. Adamovich aka "The Great Throwdini." Performed with Target Girl Barbara Adamovich.

Most Knives Thrown Around a Human Target in 1 Minute (1 knife/throw)
76. David R. Adamovich aka "The Great Throwdini." Performed with Target Girl Ekaterina Sknarina.

Most Knives Thrown Around a Human Target 1 minute (3 knives/throw)
144. David R. Adamovich aka "The Great Throwdini." Performed with Target Girl Ekaterina. Previously 102 with Target Girl Tina Nagy and 97 with Target Girl Ekaterina Sknarina.

Most Knives Thrown Around a Human Target, Ladder of Death, in 1 Minute (1 knife/throw)
74. David R. Adamovich aka "The Great Throwdini." Performed with Target Girl Kryssy Kocktail. Previously 70 with Target Girl Bonnie Swencionis aka "Bullseye."

Most Knives Thrown in 1 Minute
84. David R. Adamovich aka "The Great Throwdini."

Most Knives Thrown within 1 Second
3. David R. Adamovich aka "The Great Throwdini."

Lat Pull Down

1 Minute Total
3,960 lb. (1,800 kg). Dave Robinson.

Leg Press

1 Minute
20 kilograms: 48 repetitions. Vanessa Relph.

Letter Opening

1,000
Time: 29 minutes, 3 seconds. Ralf Laue.

Nail Catching

1 minute: 27 six-inch nails caught one at a time with

SPEED, SKILL, AND STAMINA

photo by Theresa Hong

Simon Lovell
The World's Greatest
Sleight-of-Hand Expert

50-year-old male.
Rego Park, NY, USA.
Single.
Professional entertainer and writer.
Web: www.simonlovell.com
E-mail: simon@simonlovell.com

4 World Records:

Fastest time to complete 30 total card cuts (15 each hand, simultaneously) with 1 hand doing the "Charlier" double cut: 29.25 seconds

Fastest time to complete 30 total card cuts with 1 hand doing the "Erdnase" triple cut: 1 minute, 27.56 seconds

Fastest time to complete 10 total card cuts (5 each hand, simultaneously) with 1 hand doing the "Simey" quadruple cut: 48.34 seconds

Longest running one-man, Off-Broadway show:
6 years (as of January 2010)

Simon Lovell picked up a deck of cards at the age of 4 and his grandfather taught him some simple magic tricks. It became a passion for Simon and got him into lots of trouble! After learning and working with people on the more "shady" side of life, Simon ended up as a professional card-cheat and con-man. However, he decided that wasn't the life for him and parlayed his skills into that of an entertainer using comedy and sleight-of-hand to amuse rather than steal.

Simon was very lucky to have lots of television appearances in the UK and decided in the late '80s to try his luck in America. He now lives in NYC and has the longest running one-man, Off-Broadway show in history, "Strange and Unusual Hobbies," at the SoHo Playhouse. Simon says, "Life, as ever, is a roller-coaster ride of amusement, fun, lovely women, and a beer or two along the way." A very cool thing for him was to be invited by Dr. Adamovich of Record Holders Republic to attempt a few world records at the "World Records of Magic Show." Simon's hands have never hurt so much but he proudly displays his certificates on his wall. He encourages you to try and beat him because if you do, he'll be back!

one hand. Richie Magic, catcher. David Adamovich, thrower. Distance: 14 feet.

Pancake Tossing

1 Minute
232. Dean Gould. BBC Studio London, United Kingdom on September 10, 1996.

2 Minutes
416. Ralf Laue.

5 Minutes
851. Enjays Restaurant, Leeds, United Kingdom on February 21, 2006. Dean Gould.

100 Times
Fastest: 26 seconds. Felixstowe, United Kingdom on November 5, 2005. Dean Gould.

Paper Cutting

A4 Paper
Most pieces: 10 minutes: 1,171. Amy Gould.

Para-Jumps

1 Minute
Most 45. Paddy Doyle.

100
3 minutes, 29 seconds. Stuart Barr.

1 Hour
1,850. Paddy Doyle.

5 Hours
4,921. Paddy Doyle.

7 Days
21,409. Paddy Doyle.

Playing Cards

Throwing
Furthest: 216 feet 4 inches. Lyndhurst, Ohio, USA resident, Rick Smith, Jr., broke the record for throwing a playing card the furthest on March 22, 2002 when he threw a playing card from a fresh deck of cards a distance of 216 feet 4 inches (65.94 m). Rick, a magician since the age of 7, can slice bananas in half and pierce watermelons with the cards thrown from a distance. BOAR

Unshuffling
1 hand: 38 seconds. Kapil Kalra.

2 hands: 36.16 seconds. Zdenek Bradac.

2 hands: 34.13 seconds. Zdenek Bradac. 32 Maria's playing cards, 4 suits, 7 through King.

Portrait Artist

Blindfolded
Fastest: 59.9 seconds. Gero Hilliger.

Potato Catching

Bucket
100 feet: 10 potatoes: Fastest: 37 seconds. Dean Gould, catcher, and Mark Hillman, thrower.

Pricing Gun

Fastest
1 minutes: 28 books. Alastair Galpin.

Chris McDaniel

53-year-old male.
Brooklyn, NY, USA.
Separated with no children.
Professional actor, singer, western variety artist.
Web: www.chrismcdaniel.net
E-mail: chris@chrismcdaniel.net

World Record:
Most targets cut with a bullwhip from the
hand of an assistant in 1 minute: 61

Chris McDaniel has been performing all his
life. His father was a Baptist minister and
Chris preached his first sermon at age 6.
Classically trained in vocal performance, he
has a bachelor of arts degree from Louisiana
College. After college, he performed at
Opryland USA show park in Nashville, TN,
where he had the opportunity to sing on the
world famous Grand Ole Opry with Minnie

Pearl and Roy Acuff, formed the country rock band, Palomino, in the mid '80s, and ended up mixing sound for country star Larry Gatlin and the Gatlin Brothers. Larry's role in "The Will Rogers Follies" on Broadway exposed Chris to the world of trick roping, where he discovered a passion for the western arts. Bullwhips and a one-man show followed, and that show has taken him around the world.

Chris has been seen on *The Late Show with David Letterman*, the national tours of "Annie Get Your Gun" and "The Will Rogers Follies," and regularly performs at the longest running Off-Broadway magic show, "Monday Night Magic," with world record holder, "The Great Throwdini"—Chris' inspiration, coach, and assistant for his world record attempt and one who deserves at least 90 percent of the credit for his success. Chris says he literally could not have done it without him.

Pull-ups

1 Minute, Female
31. Alicia Weber. BOAR

3 Minutes, Female
57. Alicia Weber. BOAR

30 Minutes, Female
344. Alicia Weber. BOAR

60 Minutes, Female
559. Alicia Weber. BOAR

Push-ups

1 Hour, 17 Minutes
1,001. James Clark. This was combined with performing 1,001 pull-ups within the same 1 hour, 17 minutes.

Back of Hands
5 minutes: 327. Paddy Doyle.

15 minutes: 627. Paddy Doyle.

30 minutes: 1,386. Paddy Doyle.

1 hour: 1,940. Paddy Doyle.

40 lb. backpack: 1 minute: 30. Paddy Doyle.

40 lb. backpack: 1 hour: 663. Paddy Doyle.

Fists
1,000: 18 minutes, 13 seconds. Doug Pruden.

3 hours: 5,489. Doug Pruden.

On Hens' Eggs

112. The most push-ups done on fresh hens' eggs is 112, by Johann Schneider of Austria. BOAR

One-Armed
1 minute: 114. Paddy Doyle. Tied by Doug Pruden at a later date.

10 minutes: 546. Doug Pruden.

30 minutes: 1,382. Doug Pruden.

1 hour: 2,521. Paddy Doyle.

2 hours, 30 minutes: 4,708. Paddy Doyle.

5 hours: 8,794. Paddy Doyle.

7 days: 16,723. Paddy Doyle.

Back of hand: 1 hour: 1,025. Doug Pruden.

Two-Armed
1 minute: 198. Biswaroop Roy Chowdhury. ASIA BOOK OF RECORDS

3 minutes: 190. Renata Hamplová (female record).

5 minutes: 441. Giuseppe Cusano. BOAR

10 minutes: 426. Renata Hamplová (female record).

24 hours: 37,350. Paddy Doyle.

1 year: 1,500,230. Paddy Doyle.

50 lb.: 4 hours, 30 minutes: 4,100. Paddy Doyle.

Shoulder Press

Machine

photo by Smith & Wesson

Jerry Miculek, Jr.
The World's Fastest Revolver Shooter

54-year-old male.
Princeton, LA, USA.
Married with one daughter.
Professional shooter and firearms instructor.
Web: www.bang-inc.com / E-mail: jerry@bang-inc.com

5 World Speed Shooting Records:

Fired 6 shots (each) from 10 different .38 caliber revolvers: 17.12 seconds. S&W Model 64 revolvers.

Fired 6 shots, reloaded, fired 6 shots from 1 revolver: 2.99 seconds. S&W Model 625 revolver.

Fired 8 shots from a revolver on a single target: 1.00 second. S&W Model 627 V-Comp revolver.

Fired 8 shots from a revolver on 4 targets (2 hits per target): 1.06 seconds. S&W Model 627 V-Comp revolver.

Fired 5 shots from a revolver on target: 0.57 seconds. S&W Model 64 ported barrel revolver.

Jerry Miculek, Jr. is one of the most versatile shooters in the world. He has earned dozens of national and international titles with handguns, rifles, and shotguns. What truly sets Jerry apart from the other top competitive shooters in the world are his amazing abilities with a revolver. In a sport dominated by semi-automatics, Jerry's performances with a revolver continually contradict traditional wisdom that says semi-automatics can be shot faster than revolvers. His fans in Japan have donned him, "The Revolver God." Jerry holds 4 revolver speed shooting records and has won every major revolver speed shooting competition in the world.

Jerry started shooting at local competitions in 1977. He joined the Smith & Wesson professional shooting team in 1989. Since that time, he has been a dominant force in the world of speed shooting competitions, claiming 16 consecutive wins at the International Revolver Championship. He is also reigning IPSC World Revolver Champion, USPSA National Revolver Champion, Steel Challenge World Speed Shooting Revolver Champion, IDPA National Revolver Champion, and USPSA 3-Gun Champion. Jerry has appeared on the Outdoor Network on *The American Shooter*, *Shooting USA*, and *The Shooting Gallery*. He has also been featured on the History Channel in *Tale of the Gun*, *Sharpshooters*, and *Extreme Marksman*.

16.5 lb. (7.5 kg): 1 minute: 39 repetitions. Vanessa Relph.

Sit-ups

1 Hour
2,201. James Clark.

3½ Hours
7,500. Havinder Singh.

24 Hours
44,001. James Clark.

50-lb. Weight on Chest
5 minutes: 211. Paddy Doyle.

10 minutes: 351. Paddy Doyle.

15 minutes: 501. Paddy Doyle.

30 minutes: 932. Paddy Doyle.

1 hour: 1,575. James Clark.

5 hours: 5,000. Paddy Doyle.

71-lb. Weight on Chest
121. James Clark.

Frame
5 minutes: 623. Jamie McGuire.

Skiing Machine

1 hour: 7.53 miles. Paul Woodland.

Cross-Country Skiing Machine. Distance: 4.03 miles. Time: 30 minutes. Paul Woodland.

Soap Bubble

Biggest
156 feet. Fan Yang.

Soup Can Smashing

1 minute: 23. Reed McClintock. Reed smashed 23 unopened Campbell soup cans, horizontally, over his index finger in 1 minute from a height of 1 foot.

Speed Record

4 Events
15 minutes each: 429 one-armed push-ups, 323 para-jumps, 400 squat thrusts, and 592 alternative squat thrusts. Paddy Doyle. The event is called the "Guinness Multi Fitness Challenge Record."

Squat Lifting

Most Weight
1 hour: 18,480 lb. (8,400 kg). Stuart Burrell.

Squat Thrusts

1 Minute
23. Stuart Burrell.

15 Minutes
790. Paddy Doyle.

30 Minutes
1,871. Paddy Doyle.

1 Hour
3,743. Paddy Doyle.

7 Days
21,347. Paddy Doyle.

Tina Nagy
"Target Girl Tina"

36-year-old female.
Minneapolis, MN, USA.
Single with two cats.
Accountant by day. Professional belly dancer,
target girl and bullwhip artist by night.
Web: www.tinadancer.com
www.empoweredvulnerability.com
E-mail: whipdancer@visi.com

2 World Records:

Most knives thrown around a human target
(as the target girl)

Double ladder of death (as the target girl)

Tina Nagy has been "dancing on the edge" since she left medical school in Hungary and moved to Minneapolis in 1990, where she discovered the Twin Cities' belly dance community. A long-time member of Jawaahir Dance Company, Tina is also a popular solo dancer at restaurants. As a dancer, her confidence and curiosity led her to bullwhip artist, Robert Dante, who recognized her talent for combining a sensitivity for music with a taste for dangerous circus arts. Ostensibly Robert's "assistant," Tina choreographed many parts of their acts, cracking a bullwhip herself in dual bullwhip routines.

In 2006, she met "The Great Throwdini" and performed as the knife thrower's target girl. She appeared with him on *America's Got Talent* and *Late Night with Conan O'Brien*. An accountant by day, Tina devotes her evenings to exploring aerial arts, dancing with Jawaahir and as a soloist, as well as appearing at cabarets in Minneapolis with Robert and in New York City with "The Great Throwdini" (with whom she also shares a gourmet's appreciation of culinary arts). Tina's blog at *www.EmpoweredVulnerability.com* explores what it's like to take risks, dancing on the edge of adventure—whether it's in a kitchen with friends or in front of millions of viewers on a national TV show.

Alternate
30 minutes: 1,420. Paddy Doyle.

1 hour: 2,820. Paddy Doyle.

2 hours: 4,901. Paddy Doyle.

5 hours: 6,696. Paddy Doyle.

Squats (circuit)

1 Hour
4,708. Paddy Doyle.

Squats on Fitness Ball

1 minute: 57. Stephen Buttler. BOAR

1 hour: 1,502. Stephen Buttler. BOAR

Stamp Licking

2 Minutes

ACCLAIMED AS THE WORLD'S
FASTEST AND MOST ACCURATE
KNIFE THROWER,
THE GREAT THROWDINI,
HAS SET AND BROKEN MORE WORLD
RECORDS FOR THE SPEED OF HIS
KNIFE THROWING THAN ANY OTHER
THROWER IN HISTORY!

artoon by Sean Hopkins

84. Dean Gould. Felixstowe, United Kingdom on January 2, 2006.

5 Minutes
238. On August 28, 2004, Thomas Schuster aka "Jumping Jo," set a record for licking and affixing the most postage stamps in 5 minutes. He managed to lick and affix 238 stamps to envelopes, in Ravensburg, Germany. BOAR

Most
1 minute: 57. Alastair Galpin.

Static Wall Sit (Samson's chair)

11 hours, 51 minutes, 14 seconds. Thienna Ho.

Stilt Walking

1 Hour
5.79 miles. Zdenek Jiruše of Czechoslovakia, covered 5.79 miles on stilts within 1 hour, in 1997. BOAR

1 Mile
Fastest: 7 minutes, 13 seconds. Ashrita Furman of the USA, ran a distance of 1 mile on stilts in a time of 7 minutes, 13 seconds at the Impossibility Challenger Games in Dachau, Germany on March 30, 2008. BOAR

24 Hours
76.17 miles. Zdenek Jiruše of Czechoslovakia, covered a distance of 76.17 miles on stilts within 24 hours on June 12, 1992 in Pelhrimov. BOAR

26.2 Miles
8 hours, 53 minutes, 12 seconds. In October 2001, Bill "Stretch" Coleman from Denver, Colorado,

Doug Pruden
"The Push-up Man"

45-year-old male.
Edmonton, Alberta, Canada.
Athlete specializing in fitness world records,
street performer, motivational speaker.
E-mail: push102@yahoo.ca

10 World Records in Push-ups. Among them:

Most back-of-hand push-ups in 1 hour: 1,781

Most back-of-hand, one-armed push-ups in
1 hour: 677

Most fist push-ups: 5,557 in 3 hours, 2 minutes,
30 seconds

Fastest time to complete 1,000 fist push-ups:
18 hours, 13 minutes

Most one-armed push-ups in 30 minutes: 114

Doug Pruden started doing push-ups seriously
at the age of 31 and began doing push-up shows
at Canadian fringe festivals a year later, followed

by public school appearances and talk shows 5 years later. By the age of 38, Doug began training for and eventually breaking national and world push-up records. To help promote push-ups, his favorite thing is to do push-up demonstrations in the community. Having set or broken 10 world records makes Doug an interesting guest on television, for example: *Open Mike with Mike Bullard*, *The Big Breakfast Show* on A-Channel in Canada, CBC's *Undercurrents*, *CTV National News* feature story on *Guinness World Records™*, and *News Hour* on Global Edmonton.

Doug has also been featured or included in numerous international Internet sites: *The Guinness Book World Records*, *The Book of Alternative Records*, *Alberta Views*, *The National Post*—Canada, *The Globe and Mail*—Canada, *Zivot* magazine—Slovakia, and on Edmonton radio shows. His heart remains where it all began—push-up shows at Canadian fringe theatre festivals and doing motivational talks at public schools, nationally and eventually around the world. Doug's humbled to say that because of his world records and motivational talks, many people now indicate to him that they include push-ups as part of their own healthy workout routine.

USA, walked the Dublin, Ireland Marathon, 26.2 miles, while wearing stilts, in a time of 8 hours, 53 minutes, 12 seconds, beating his previous record by one and a half hours. BOAR

Most People to Simultaneously Walk on Stilts
625. Doug Hunt. Doug Hunt organized a mass stilt walk of 625 people walking 328 feet (100 m) on 12-inch peg stilts.

Tallest
56 feet 6 inches. Roy Maloy. Roy, while wearing an overhead safety wire, took 5 independent steps on 56-foot, 6-inch aluminum stilts weighing 50.6 lb. each.

Tallest / Heaviest
50 feet 9 inches weighing 68.5 lb. each. Doug Hunt took 29 independent steps on the world's heaviest and tallest stilts.

Talking

Fastest
1 second: 11 words. Fran Capo of Putnam Valley, NY, USA, was recorded speaking 603.32 words in 54.2 seconds (11 words per second). This occurred in Las Vegas on June 5, 1990.

Tennis

Ball Bouncing on Edge of Racket
1 minute: 215. Dean Gould. Magnum Spedition Offices, Felixstowe, United Kingdom on June 4, 1999.

Throat Strikes

Left Arm

30 seconds: 67. Paddy Doyle.

Right Arm
30 seconds: 68. Paddy Doyle.

Throwing

Billiard Cue
Distance: 141.4 feet. The greatest recorded distance that a billiard cue has been thrown javelin fashion is 141.4 feet, by Dan Kornblum of Germany, in Flensburg, Germany in 1998. BOAR

Compact Disc
Distance: 218.99 feet. Kim Flatow.

Toilet Plunger
90 Seconds: 30. Gerhard Donie. Plunger remained against board for at least 3 seconds. BOAR

Vinyl Disc Record
Distance: 477.4 feet: The distance record for throwing a vinyl record is 477.40 feet, held by Axel Schulz of Germany. BOAR

Tiles

Broken with Punch
2 minutes: 280. Jitendra Sharma. ASIA BOOK OF RECORDS

Treadmill

Marathon
2 hours, 23 minutes, 58 seconds. Eric Blake. BOAR

Team of 12
Time: 24 hours. Distance: 261.75 miles. Average pace: 5.30 mph.

Peter Rosendahl
The World's Fastest Unicyclist

40-year-old male.
Sweden / Germany.
Married with three children.
Professional entertainer, world record breaking
unicyclist, master instructor in martial arts,
president of the European Budo Council.
Web: www.peter-rosendahl.eu
E-mail: peterrosendahl67@aol.com

World Records on Unicycle. Among them:

Fastest 100 meter unicycle sprint: 11.43 seconds

Fastest skip roping in 1 minute: 213 times

Smallest rideable unicycle:
14.8 mm wheel

Jumping most stairs upward:
525 stairs in 9 minutes, 27 seconds;
56 stairs in 30 seconds

Backward unicycling: 75 kilometers in 9 hours

Peter Rosendahl is best known as the fastest unicyclist in the world, and has devoted his life to riding the unicycle and training in martial arts (Budo). Peter was born in Köping, Sweden in 1967. His father, a great man and magician, influenced him. He introduced and trained Peter to be a great motorcyclist and horseback rider. He also introduced Peter to unicycling at the age of 7. Peter set his first world record at the age of 12. He's been traveling around the world performing for most of his life, performing in over 40 countries and appearing on over 200 TV shows.

In 35 years of performing, Peter has set and/or broken over 40 world records. One of his greatest accomplishments is to have headlined at many hotels and casinos in Las Vegas, the entertainment capital of the world. When he's not performing, Peter often appears as a guest lecturer in martial art camps around the world and serves as the President of the European Budo Council. Today, he mostly works with his show around the world in different TV and special show productions, and between that, he headlines as a guest entertainer on world famous cruise ships on the seven seas.

100 Miles
13 hours, 42 minutes, 33 seconds. Suresh Joachim.

62 Miles (100 km)
7 hours, 21 minutes, 40 seconds. Suresh Joachim.

1 Week
Furthest: 409.65 miles. Suresh Joachim.

Unicycle

Distance
4.34 miles (7 km). Time: 22 minutes on a 24-inch unicycle. Peter Rosendahl.

328-foot (100 m) sprint with a standstill start: 12.11 seconds. Peter Rosendahl.

328-foot (100 m) sprint with a flying start: 11.43 seconds. Peter Rosendahl.

Time: 13 hours. Distance: 70 miles (113 km). Peter Rosendahl.

Jumping Most Stairs Upward
525 stairs upward (consecutive jumps): 9 minutes, 27 seconds. Peter Rosendahl.

Riding Backward Long Distance on Time
46.5 miles (75 km) backward in 9 hours, 25 minutes. Peter Rosendahl.

Rope Skipping
213 consecutive times in 1 minute. Peter Rosendahl.

Smallest Ridable
15 mm wheel, 30 cm high. Distance: 6.43 meters. Peter Rosendahl.

16 mm wheel, 30 cm high. Distance: 20 meters. Peter Rosendahl.

33 mm wheel with no chain, 25 cm high. Distance: 6 meters. Peter Rosendahl.

Weight Catch

Caught from a Distance of 10 Feet
57.2 lb. Fred Burton. Weight thrown by Peter Johnson.

Whip Cracking

Paper Plate
1 minute: 23. Ari Lauanne. Ari hit twenty-three 9-inch paper plates mid-air in 1 minute using a 7-foot total length bullwhip (5-foot bullwhip plus 2-foot fall/cracker). The plates were tossed by Ari and handed to him by an assistant.

Target in Assistant's Hand
1 minute: 61. Chris McDaniel. Chris cracked sixty-one 8-inch targets from an assistant's hand in 1 minute using a 6-foot 1¾-inch bullwhip, from butt to tip.

Double Volley
15 second: 112. Chris McDaniel. Four foot bullwhip with a 26" fall, one in each hand.

Window Cleaning

3 Standard Windows
9.24 seconds. Terry Burrows.

Winkle Picking

50 Picked
1 minute, 22.4 seconds. Dean Gould.

Justin Style
"James Bond with a Stack of Coins"

48-year-old male.
East Hanover, NJ, USA.
Single.
Professional magician and sleight-of-hand artist.
Web: www.myspace.com/justinstylemagic
E-mail: justinstyle1@aol.com

3 World Records:

One-handed production of 8 US Silver dollars:
25.41 seconds

One-handed production of 9 US Silver dollars:
30.66 seconds

One-handed production of 10 US Silver dollars:
34.88 seconds

Justin Style always loved coin magic and has profound respect for sleight-of-hand magicians. When he first started performing magic, people would tell Justin they liked his magic and thought they never saw a true master to compare him against. As he began studying, Justin found a book on coin magic. Once he began reading, he never stopped practicing. Justin studied the past masters, such as T. Nelson Downs, who was known around the world as the "King of Koins," during the early twentieth century and created the "Downs Palm." It was this technique that Justin learned and developed over the years. Now, he is able to hold and produce 10 US Silver dollars in a single Downs Palm.

Justin dedicates his records to the great coin artists around the world. His greatest achievement was when he performed this routine for a room of 250 of the world's best close-up magicians at the world renowned Fechter's Finger Flicking Frolic. Being part of the Record Holder's Republic is truly a highlight of his career. It was a proud moment for him that day in New York City! You can see Justin perform close-up magic at "Monday Night Magic" in NYC.

Set in 1 Hour
14. Paddy Doyle. World Cup Competition, April 18, 2007.

Yo-Yo

Consecutive Suicides
42. David Geigle of Germany, performed 42 on October 28, 2006 at the German Masters Yo-Yo Championship. He used a Dark Magic by Yo-Yo Jam. Supplied and verified by the American Yo-Yo Association.

Eli Hops
120. David Schulte of the USA, performed 120 on July 28, 2005 at the World Yo-Yo Championship in Orlando, Florida, aged 35. He used a Bare Bones by Dif-e-Yo. Supplied and verified by the American Yo-Yo Association.

Freehand Shoulder Pop
48. Nathan Christy of the USA, performed 48 on October 7, 2006 at the National Yo-Yo Championship in Chico, California, aged 21. He used a Night Moves by Yo-Yo Jam. Supplied and verified by the American Yo-Yo Association.

Iron Whips
193. Brett Ferante performed 193 on August 10, 2006 at the World Yo-Yo Championship in Orlando, Florida. He used a Dark Magic by Yo-Yo Jam. Supplied and verified by the American Yo-Yo Association.

Longest Sleeper: Fixed Axle to Extinction
3 minutes, 23.11 seconds. Tim Redmond of the USA, performed for 3 minutes, 23.11 seconds at the Maryland State Yo-Yo Championship, aged 31. He

used a DJ by Yo-Yo Jam. Supplied and verified by the American Yo-Yo Association.

Longest Shoot the Moon: String Length (3 repeats)
13 feet 2 inches. Dave Schulte of the USA, performed with a string length of 13 feet 2 inches on August 10, 2006 at the World Yo-Yo Championship in Orlando, Florida. He use an Aquarius by Yo-Yo Jam. Supplied and verified by the American Yo-Yo Association.

Longest Sleeper: Transaxle to Extinction
16 minutes, 17.18 seconds. Tim Redmond of the USA, performed for 16 minutes, 17.18 seconds, on May 28, 2005 at the Pennsylvania State Yo-Yo Championship, aged 30. He used a Yo-Yo Jam Mega Spin Factor 2.2. Supplied and verified by the American Yo-Yo Association.

Loops and Punching Bag
256. Joseph Harris of the USA, performed 256 on October 7, 2006 at the United States National Yo-Yo Championship in Chico, California, aged 19. He used a Sunset Trajectories by Yo-Yo Jam. Supplied and verified by the American Yo-Yo Association.

Milk the Cow
562. Bill de Boisblanc of the USA, performed 562 on August 10, 2006 at the World Yo-Yo Championship in Orlando, Florida, aged 65. He used a Sunset Trajectories by Yo-Yo Jam. Supplied and verified by the American Yo-Yo Association.

Off-string Whips
146. Jimmy Peng of the USA, performed 146 on August 10, 2006 at the World Yo-Yo Champion-

Tim Waterson

47-year-old male.
Edmonton, Alberta, Canada.
Professional drummer, educator, author, and clinician.
Web: www.timwaterson.net
www.myspace.com/timwaterson
E-mail: timwaterson@hotmail.com

3 World Records as the World's Fastest
Drummer for the Feet:

Fastest single pedal roll played on a bass drum in 60 seconds: 650 strokes

Fastest single stroke roll played on a bass drum in 60 seconds: 1,057 strokes

Fastest double stroke roll played on a bass drum in 60 seconds: 1,407 strokes

Tim Waterson has been performing as a drummer in a variety of bands since the age of 16. He created the world record for the world's fastest drummer for the feet in June

2000 by becoming the first drummer in history to play over 1,000 strokes in 60 seconds, on *The Big Breakfast* morning TV show in Edmonton, Canada, and this was verified by the World's Fastest Drummer Organization using the Guinness certified drumometer. Tim was also featured on the Discovery Channel's *Extreme Body Parts* program and set a *new* record of 1,153 in double strokes in 2001.

In November 2002, he was a featured performer at the Montreal Drum Fest and set another double stroke record of 1,289 strokes in 60 seconds. In 2002, at Musicians Institute in Hollywood, Tim once again broke his own record, with 1,407 in double strokes in 60 seconds. Ever since he created the world record for drumming, Tim has been performing at drum trade shows and drum clinics at music stores. He also released two instructional DVDs detailing the so-called secrets to achieving world record speeds and explaining the techniques, motions, and applications for bass drum playing.

ship in Orlando, Florida, aged 19. He used a Special Agent by Yo-Yo Jam. Supplied and verified by the American Yo-Yo Association.

One-Handed Behind the Back Loops
581. Tomonari Ishiguro of Japan, performed 581 on August 6, 2004 at the World Yo-Yo Championship in Orlando, Florida. He used a Bandi Hyper Raider by Yomega. Supplied and verified by the American Yo-Yo Association.

Punching Bag
321. Luke Roberts of England, performed 321 on August 10, 2006 at the World Yo-Yo Championship in Orlando, Florida, aged 22. He used a Raiders by Yomega. Supplied and verified by the American Yo-Yo Association.

Regenerated Trapezius
224. David Schulte of the USA, performed 224 on June 17, 2005 at the Midwest Regional in Minnesota, aged 35. He used a Hyperwarp Heavy Wings by Yomega. Supplied and verified by the American Yo-Yo Association.

Ride the Horse
250. Luke Roberts of England, performed 250 on July 28, 2005 at the World Championship in Orlando, Florida, aged 21. He used a Raiders by Yomega. Supplied and verified by the American Yo-Yo Association.

Shoot the Moon
1,057. Bill de Boisblanc of the USA, performed 1,057, on July 28, 2005 at the World Yo-Yo Championship in Orlando, Florida, aged 64. He used a Dragon Jams

by Yo-Yo Jam. Supplied and verified by the American Yo-Yo Association.

Two-Handed Inside Loops
540. Bill de Boisblanc of the USA, performed 540 on October 5, 2007 at the National Yo-Yo Championship in Chico, CA, aged 67. He used two Sunset Trajectories by Yo-Yo Jam. Supplied and verified by the American Yo-Yo Association.

Two-Handed Outside Loops
250. Dale Myrberg of the USA, performed 250 on July 18, 2006 at the World Yo-Yo Championship in Rapid City, South Dakota, aged 54. He used standard fixed axle Russell Yo-Yos. Supplied and verified by the American Yo-Yo Association.

Whirlwind
599. Luke Roberts of England, performed 599 on August 10, 2006 at the World Yo-Yo Championship in Orlando, Florida, aged 22. He used a Hyper Raiders by Yomega. Supplied and verified by the American Yo-Yo Association.

Conclusion

With all the human achievement world records listed in *Believe the Unbelievable,* we've stayed away from all the popular sporting records on purpose. The Olympics and yearly world championships in swimming as well as track-and-field are consistently monitored, with a long history of record keeping on their own. But to use them as examples in this discourse is perfect fodder for discussion.

The progression of three world records familiar to most everyone—and in the limelight every four years with each summer Olympics—are the 100-meter dash, the 100-meter freestyle swim, and the 1-mile run. Only the men's records are shown and represent what we know as the "fastest man on earth," for both running and swimming. The women's results follow a similar path and are but a fraction slower than the men's records—the reasons for which are entirely a different matter of debate and will not be discussed here.

Breaking the "4 minute mile" by Dr. Roger Bannister, for example, stands as one of the most monumental records of all-time. Was it possible? Why yes, of course! In each event, the improvement in the second half of its recorded history has decreased or been less than in the first half. Are we approaching a plateau in improvement? Are we approaching the absolute of human speed? You be the judge. Undoubtedly, improvements in sport science, diet, training, conditioning, track and pool design, running shoes and swimming suits have all had their impacts. But when all is said and done, it comes down to man versus man. With everything else being equal, *the* fastest man will arrive at the finish line first—albeit by 1/100th or possibly 1/1000th of a second. Period.

The results:

100-meter Sprint
In 1912 the record was 10.6 seconds. The current record, set in 2008, is 9.69 seconds.

In 96 years, the record has fallen 0.91 seconds, or 0.01 seconds/year.

In the first half of that period, the record fell 0.6 seconds, or 0.013 seconds/year.

In the second half of that period, the record fell 0.31 seconds, or 0.006 seconds/year.

100-meter Freestyle Swim

In 1905 the record was 1 minute, 5.8 seconds. The current record, set in 2008, is 47.05 seconds.

In 103 years, the record has fallen 18.75 seconds, or 0.18 seconds/year.

In the first half of that period, the record fell 10.4 seconds, or 0.20 seconds/year.

In the second half of that period, the record fell 8.35 seconds, or 0.16 seconds/year.

1-mile Run

In 1913 the record was 4 minutes, 14.1 seconds. The current record, set in 1999, is 3 minutes, 43.13 seconds.

In 86 years, the record has fallen 30.97 seconds, or 0.36 seconds/year.

In the first half of that period, the record fell 16.9 seconds, or 0.39 seconds/year.

In the second half of that period, the record fell 14.07 seconds, or 0.34 seconds/year.

So how do the speed numbers look in some of the *Believe the Unbelievable* records? I can address those most familiar to me: my own in knife throwing, the balloon records of Thomas Blacke, and beer-mat flipping records of Dean Gould, in addition to several other mind-boggling displays of speed and agility. The question still remains, can they be beat or are we approaching the limits of human achievement?

Fast knife throwing comes about under two circumstances: the Wheel of Death in performance and in the stopwatch world of record setting and breaking. The fastest performances I've seen with the Wheel of Death—throwing two knives per revolution while spinning a human target on a revolving wheel—have been by Kenny Pierce (Che Che Whitecloud), Fritz Brumbach, Pat Brumbach (Fritz' son), "The Great Throwdini" (myself), and others such as Marroni and Tyrone Lanier. All of these professional knife throwers do The Wheel, give or take a few hundredths of a second, at 1.1 second per revolution, throwing 2 knives per revolution or consecutive knives at 0.55 seconds each. Obviously the limits of this stunt are dictated by what becomes a reasonable versus an inhuman or reckless speed to spin a human target in light of the extremely small margin of error. A knife thrown just 0.1 second too early or too late could mean disaster as the helpless target girl suddenly finds herself in the wrong place at the wrong time! We won't go there.

As it relates to record setting, there are two prominent speed knife-throwing record breakers in the world today, "The Great Throwdini" and Pat Brumbach. Each is capable of sticking 3 knives in the board within 1 second (half spin from approximately 7 feet from the board using 13 to 14 inch professional throwing knives). Throwdini's latest record is throwing ten 14-inch throwing knives from the command *go* to successfully sticking the tenth knife in 3.73 seconds. This amounts to a cycle time of approximately 0.4 seconds per knife. In other words, there is a *thunk* at the board every 0.4 seconds as the knives are "fired" from hand to board. The time to reach the board has been filmed at 60 frames per second with digital videography and found to be 0.15 second (or 0.05 second per quarter turn of the knife). The time to blindly grab the knife from the hand holding the stack of knives to swing and throw is less than 1/2 second. That's fast!

This discussion, of course, relates to the frequency of throwing and not the speed (velocity) at which the thrown knife moves from hand to board. High-speed digital videography has shown velocity to range from 26–32 miles per hour—the former when throwing for frequency and the latter when throwing "hard." For a thrown object, this might be considered slow in comparison to a professional baseball pitch thrown around 90 miles per hour. But one is a 12 ounce, 14-inch length of steel with a point that's rotating through the air end-over-end, and the other is a 4-ounce ball spinning through the air. The forces of physics and the methods thrown are entirely different despite some very minor similarities in the throwing motion. In either case, you wouldn't be on the receiving end of a misthrown knife or misthrown baseball. Both will *hurt*, unfortunately the receiver and not the thrower.

Dean Gould, "The World's Most Dexterous Man," is known for the speed at which he can balance stacks of items on his elbow and then suddenly let them fall only to be caught by the same hand of that arm in just tenths of a second. In fact, high-speed digital videography has shown Dean to drop and catch a stack of beermats in 0.23 seconds, from the moment his elbow begins the drop to the time his open hand makes contact with the stack. In other words, in just one-quarter second after "unloading" the stack of beermats from his elbow, the stack has dropped perhaps 8 inches and his outstretched fingers are already clamping down around the stack, open palm facing away from his body with his thumb under and his fingers above the stack. That's fast!

Thomas Blacke entered the world record-breaking scene in 2006 at Record Holders Republic first "World Records of Magic Show" at Fantasma Magic in NYC. Thomas was there to set the world record for balloon dog sculpting. In a brilliant display of speed, dexterity and showmanship, magician and escape artist Thomas Blacke had set two new world records: front of body dog sculpture in 4.18 seconds and rear of body dog sculpture in 4.35 seconds. The command *go* was given by RHR official timer Chris McDaniel, and in the blink of an eye and a few squeaks later, there appeared a balloon dog. The audience broke into a resounding applause in utter astonishment. Thomas has since broken his front of body dog sculpting down to 3.10 seconds. That's fast!

Pistol shooter Jerry Miculek holds 5 records for the speed of his shooting a revolver and reloading. Imagine the dexterity and speed by which his trigger finger is moving to fire six shots, reload, and fire another six shots from one revolver in 2.99 seconds, using a Smith and Wesson Model 625 revolver. That's a total of 12 bullets fired in two bursts of 6 each with one reload in less than 3 seconds. That's fast!

Likewise, there are records and displays of speed that are as astonishing in another way, for instance, the ability to move your arm through the air and snatch a lethal object approaching you, e.g., Throwdini's knife catch, and Larry Cisewski's arrow catch (not a world record but an incredible feat). Throwdini has developed the technique to stand before another knife thrower throwing 14-inch knives for one full spin from 12 feet away and snatch the knife midair as it comes speeding in at around 25 miles per hour. The world record, held by Throwdini, is 25 knives in 1 minute (30 were thrown and 5 were dropped). Larry Cisewski, a professional knife thrower and arrow catcher, stands approximately 30 feet from an archer using a 35 lb. test bow, shooting an arrow toward a bull's-eye at 70 feet per second. Larry stands near the target, turns and snatches the arrow right out of the air. And then there's world record holder and martial artist Ed Byrne, whose karate chop has been measured at 6 meters per second. That's fast!

Whip cracking is a fascinating skill of speed and dexterity. World record holder and world champion Chris McDaniel has displayed a speed and accuracy record worthy of discussion: Cutting 61 targets out of an assistant's hand in 1 minute. That's just better than one crack per second in which a handheld target was hit with a 6-foot bullwhip. It's clear the limits of speed and accuracy are being approached as arm and hand muscles are pushing their limits. That's fast!

The most prolific endurance event world record holder is Paddy Doyle, known as "The World's Fittest Endurance Athlete." Paddy holds records in martial arts as well, for example, 29,850 full contact punch strikes in 1 hour. This gives new meaning to the term "pummeling your opponent" as strikes are coming in faster than 8 per second, non-stop, for 1 hour. Ouch. That's fast!

One must wonder if there are limits to human performance. In sporting events such as the 100-meter sprint, the 100-meter freestyle swim, and the 1-mile run, the rate of improvement appears to be on the decline, in other words, a minor plateau is occurring as the limits of human speed are approached. It's illogical to think that if you follow the curve it will eventually reach "zero." Will electronic scoring have to go out to thousandths of a second? Will human achievement speed world records ever cease to be broken? Are records really meant to be broken? Can they be broken forever?

Just how fast is fast? Just how long is long? Perhaps you'll have a chance to find out for yourself by appearing in one of RHR's TV specials, *The Make It or Break It World Record Show*, in which the drama of competing for a world record culminates in either the making or breaking of a new or existing world record. Updates for the show will appear at *www .recordholdersrepublic.com*.

Moreover, we end this book with an open challenge for someone, anyone, to do the "RHR Going

The Extra Mile Challenge" record. On May 29, 2009, 11:30 p.m. and finishing July 10, 2009, at approximately 2:30 p.m., Richard Dunwoody, MBE, walked 1,000 miles in 1,000 hours, walking 1 mile in *every* hour for 1,000 *consecutive* hours; that's 24 miles in 24 hours (almost a marathon a day) for 42 days and nights, with only 1 hour, 15 minutes sleep possible at any one time—if he walks back to back miles in different hours. This miraculous feat was first performed by Captain Robert Barclay Allardice in 1809. In essence, the "RHR Going The Extra Mile Challenge" record would be to complete 1,001 miles in 1,000 consecutive hours by walking no less than 1 mile in each of 1,000 consecutive hours.

David R. Adamovich, Ed.D.

David R. Adamovich, Ed.D. (Former Professor of Sports Sciences and Fellow of the American College of Sports Medicine). Dr. Adamovich performs professionally as an impalement artist and is the world's fastest knife thrower.

Make It or Break It

These are the things you will need if you are serious about setting or breaking a world record.

Human Achievement (like the records in *Believe the Unbelievable*):
- Record Holders Republic
  (*www.recordholdersrepublic.co.uk*)
- The Book of Alternative Records
  (*www.recordholders.org*)
- Guinness World Records™
  (*www.guinnessworldrecords.com*)

Collection Record—largest, smallest:
- The Book of Alternative Records
  (*www.recordholders.org*)
- Guinness World Records™
  (*www.guinnessworldrecords.com*)

Carefully and extensively search the internet and world record books to see if the record already exists. If not, then contact the organization you want to have your record registered with and state you'd like to SET a NEW record. See if there is a pre-submission form or application to complete. State your case clearly. Specify exactly what you want to do. If the record does exist, then be sure to include that information in your request. Specify the record and who has it.

Once approved, plan all the logistics:
• How will it be recorded?
• Who will the witnesses will be?
• Are the witnesses capable of accurately recording the record?
• "Engineer" the record by running through it, seeing what can be improved and what practice you're going to need to make a successful attempt.
• Follow through with the organization as soon as possible. (Someone else may be working on the same thing without your knowledge.)

Forms used by Record Holders Republic are at: *www.recordholdersrepublic.co.uk/rhrsubmissionform.pdf*

Everyone has a particular talent. It may be good enough to set or break a world record. You won't know until you try. Creativity is paramount to setting a new record. Are you getting the message? Be creative. Go for it. Become a world record holder.

RECORD HOLDERS REPUBLIC
Registry of Official World Records[tm]
Dean Gould (U.K.), Founder. (The Rev. Dr.) David R. Adamovich (U.S.)

The mission of the Record Holders Republic 'Registry of Official World Records' is to standardize the definition, authentication, registration, and organization of Official World Records with respect to time, distance, and amount, or any other quality so defining world records. The Registry will serve as a clearing house for records collated and reported by Record Holders Republic (recordholdersrepublic.co.uk), and Believe The Unbelievable! (Bartleby Press, 2010).

RECORD SUBMISSION FORM

Your Name: _____ Phone _____ E-Mail _____

Address: _____

Web site: _____ DOB (mm/dd/yyyy): _____

Part I. Record Holder's Statement — Proposed Name of Record (for example: The Most 6" Pancakes Flipped in One Minute, The Most Dominos Balanced on One Domino, The Fastest Drum Beats in One Minute, The Most Sit Ups in One Hour).

_____

Is this a NEW record (never done before)? _____, OR Is this the BREAKING of an existing record? _____.
If BREAKING provide details of who holds the record, when done, where recorded, the details of the record, and how your attempt will break that record. Record Holders Republic believes, "Records are made to be broken" — provided they are done under the same or similar conditions!

Held by: Recorded by (RHR, Guinness™, etc.):

Date: Where:

Details:

_____

_____

_____

Part II. Record Facts — **Describe in detail** the facts of your submission. Include all measurements, times, etc.

Date of Event: Location of Event:

What did you do?:

_____

_____

_____

_____

NOTE: If this is a NEW record attach a Rules/Guidelines page giving the specifics, in detail, of what what used, how, etc.

Part III. Documentation — The more documentation included the easier it will be to decide if world record status can be awarded. For example: video (PAL in the UK, NTSC in the US), DVD, photos, newspaper clippings, TV/media coverage, and 2 witness statements (see Witness Statement Form). In submitting the information I understand that Record Holders Republic (RHR) is not obligated to designate World Record status to my submission as that decision is based on their belief in **supporting evidence** and/or **relevence** of my claim. RHR's policy is to seek records that are reproducible, breakable and based on skill. Freak, strange and unusual anomilies are not world records. "Stunts" involving luck or uncontrolled danger should not be submitted. Upon acceptance an Official RHR World Record Certificate is available. Submission to RHR web database is guaranteed. I have read and understand the above statement and attest that the information provided is true and accurate.

Signed: _____ Date: _____

SAMPLE

RECORD HOLDERS REPUBLIC
Registry of Official World Records[tm]
Dean Gould (U.K.), Founder. (The Rev. Dr.) David R. Adamovich (U.S.)

The mission of the Record Holders Republic 'Registry of Official World Records' is to standardize the definition, authentication, registration, and organization of Official World Records with respect to time, distance, and amount, or any other quality so defining world records. The Registry will serve as a clearing house for records collated and reported by Record Holders Republic (recordholdersrepublic.co.uk), and Believe The Unbelievable! (Bartleby Press, 2010).

WITNESS A STATEMENT FORM

Name of Person Submitting Record: _____ Date: _____

Name of Proposed Record: _____

Witness Name: _____ Phone _____ E-Mail _____

Address: _____

Position and/or relevence to record: _____

The person named above is submitting a world record attempt to The Record Holders Republic Registry of Official World Records. By completing this form you are attesting the information provided is true and accurate, that you witnessed the event and there is no reason to believe what was witnessed was anything other than stated, i.e., there is no evidence of deceit and that any apparatus involved was not gaffed or rigged in any fashion.

Describe in your own words and in detail the event so witnessed (date, time, conditions, outcome, etc.): _____

_____

_____

_____

_____

_____

_____

_____

_____

_____

_____

Signed: _____ Date: _____

Note to person attempting record. Make back-up copies of all material submitted. We will keep accepted record information on file. Declined record information will be returned provided return postage is received upon request. If you are **NOT in the United States** send your statement, the witness statements and all documentation to Mr. Dean Gould, 21 Church Road, High Road East, Old Felixstowe, Suffolk, IP119NF, UK. If you are in the **United States** send all material to Dr. David R. Adamovich, 876 Guy Lombardo Avenue, Freeport, NY 11520. You will receive two e-mails in a timely fashion: the first to confirm receipt of your submission and the second to inform you our decision. If accepted you will be given the opportunity to receive one or more Official Certificates designating your Registry number and World Record Status. Thank you for your support of Record Holders Republic. We wish you the best with all your world record attempts, now and in the future.

Dean Gould / David Adamovich

RECORD HOLDERS REPUBLIC
Registry of Official World Records^{tm}
Dean Gould (U.K.), Founder. (The Rev. Dr.) David R. Adamovich (U.S.)

The mission of the Record Holders Republic 'Registry of Official World Records' is to standardize the definition, authentication, registration, and organization of Official World Records with respect to time, distance, and amount, or any other quality so defining world records. The Registry will serve as a clearing house for records collated and reported by Record Holders Republic (recordholdersrepublic.co.uk), and Believe The Unbelievable! (Bartleby Press, 2010).

WITNESS B STATEMENT FORM

Name of Person Submitting Record: _____ Date: _____

Name of Proposed Record: _____

Witness Name: _____ Phone _____ E-Mail _____

Address: _____

Position and/or relevence to record: _____

The person named above is submitting a world record attempt to The Record Holders Republic Registry of Official World Records. By completing this form you are attesting the information provided is true and accurate, that you witnessed the event and there is no reason to believe what was witnessed was anything other than stated, i.e., there is no evidence of deceit and that any apparatus involved was not gaffed or rigged in any fashion.

Describe in your own words and in detail the event so witnessed (date, time, conditions, outcome, etc.):

_____

_____

_____

_____

_____

_____

_____

_____

_____

_____

_____

Signed: _____ Date: _____

Note to person attempting record. Make back-up copies of all material submitted. We will keep accepted record information on file. Declined record information will be returned provided return postage is received upon request. If you are **NOT in the United States** send your statement, the witness statements and all documentation to Mr. Dean Gould, 21 Church Road, High Road East, Old Felixstowe, Suffolk, IP119NF, UK. If you are in the **United States** send all material to Dr. David R. Adamovich, 876 Guy Lombardo Avenue, Freeport, NY 11520. You will receive two e-mails in a timely fashion: the first to confirm receipt of your submission and the second to inform you our decision. If accepted you will be given the opportunity to receive one or more Official Certificates designating your Registry number and World Record Status. Thank you for your support of Record Holders Republic. We wish you the best with all your world record attempts, now and in the future.

Dean Gould / David Adamovich

Afterword

YOU'RE JUST NOT GOING TO BELIEVE THIS

What better way to close *Believe the Unbelievable* than with some world record business that falls in the category of "You're just not going to believe this!"

From the world's largest store: "Thank you for your kind offer of a certificate declaring Macy's the world's largest store. As you can imagine we have very limited office space and must decline your offer."

What?

⸺⬥⸺

From a hotel in the United Arab Emirates offering the world's most expensive hotel stay, $1,000,000 for one week: "Thank you very much for your in-

terest to Emirates Palace, with regards to your below proposal to include our record in your book, we
would like to know if this is free of charge."

*We guess times are tough, even in the United Arab
Emirates.*

———◆———

From a well-known world record organization:
"We're unable to accept your claim of 'Most Knives
Caught in One Minute: 25,' and suggest you try to
break another record, 'Most Knives Thrown Around
a Human Target in One Minute: 102,' currently held
by David Adamovich."

*Did the person writing that e-mail bother to notice
they were corresponding with David Adamovich?*

Doesn't it make you want to shake your head
and say, "You've got to *Believe the Unbelievable,* too!"
You couldn't possibly make this stuff up.

———◆———

By now, you've probably admired (a few times)
the amazing illustration of Record Holder, John Evans
(profile on page 21) that was created especially for
the front cover of *Believe the Unbelievable.*

The cover was produced by award-winning artist, Ralph Butler. Look closely. It was actually paint-
ed on a piece of wood.

We're confidant that you may have seen Ralph's
work before. Or, at least, you may have held it your

 hand. After all, it was reproduced about *800 million* times. You see, Ralph Butler designed the back on the Florida state quarter that was released in 2004.

Sort of gives new meaning to the expression "right on the money," doesn't it?

Record Holders Republic (RHR) Team

Presidents:

Dean Gould, Founder

USA

David R. Adamovich,
  Ed.D.

Vice Presidents:

UK

John Evans

Peter Dowdeswell

USA

Thomas Blacke

India

Kapil Kalra

Krishan Chahal

Biswaroop Roy

George Bernard

Navneet Singh

Nitin Grover

Manish Mishra

Vijay Patnaik

Sachin Kumar, Ph.D.

Canada

Doug Pruden

Don Williamson

Advisory Panel:

UK

Creighton Carvello

USA
Thomas Blacke
Collen Fitzpatrick,
    Ph.D.
Simon Lovell
Bill SanRoman,
    M.D., F.A.C.C.
George Shea
Richard Shea

Dan Meyer

Motivational Coaches:
Ricardo Bellino
Fran Capo

Representers:
Tim Fitzhigham
Alastair Galpin